More Nuggets of Wisdom

Quotes to Ponder and Inspire

Compiled by Brent N. Hunter

Spirit Rising Productions

ISBN: 978-0-9858821-5-0
Library of Congress Control Number: 2013919802
Edition: First
Format: Hardcover
Publication Date: February 1, 2014

Spirit Rising Productions
2261 Market Street, Suite 637
San Francisco, CA 94114

Visit our website at www.SpiritRising.TV

Cover art by Mark Janssen (www.janssen-designs.com)

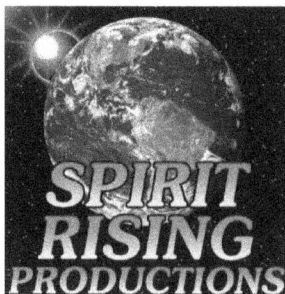

Dedication

As an unknown wise person once said, "we do not inherit the earth from our ancestors, we borrow it from our children". This book is dedicated to children and people of young spirit, to whom we owe our best efforts at leaving the world better than we found it.

This book is also dedicated to my mother, Isçe Güner Gökcen Hunter, and father, Jack Nathan Hunter, who each helped make the world better in their own unique and special loving ways.

Acknowledgements

Grateful acknowledgment is given to the sources of quotes in this book, all of whom have been identified to the greatest extent possible.

In addition, I want to thank my beloved Dea Shandera, who patiently provided loving and brilliant suggestions throughout the production of this book.

Finally, I want to thank my friend and colleague David Christel for his exceptional expertise with editing, page layout, formatting, quote source verification and for his eagle eye attention to detail.

Table of Contents

Introduction

We live in an infinite universe. It is irresponsible to be pessimistic in a field of infinite possibilities, and therefore, it is our responsibility to attempt to be positive in every situation in which we find ourselves. When we are guided by using the most inspiring and uplifting interpretation of any situation or experience, we will always be led towards the most positive outcome.

Let us be guided by our ideals, as we navigate the waters of life in the early 21st century. May this book of quotes remind us of our ideals, and may it help uplift and inspire us through these changing times.

During the course of posting a variety of inspiring and engaging quotes on social media for more than a decade, people have asked if I had all of the quotes available in a single place. In addition to *Nuggets of Wisdom*, this *More Nuggets of Wisdom* book brings together many of the quotes I've collected over the years, as well as some of my own messages. If you would like to see these inspiring quotes and messages on a daily basis via social media, connect with me on Twitter at twitter.BrentHunter.TV, on Facebook at facebook.BrentHunter.TV, LinkedIn at linkedin.BrentHunter.TV, YouTube at youtube.BrentHunter.TV, Instagram at instagram.BrentHunter.TV and Pinterest at pinterest.BrentHunter.TV or at SpiritRising.TV .

I'm happy you've found this book and hope you'll carry these nuggets of wisdom close to your heart.

Enjoy!

Brent N. Hunter
January 7, 2014
West Hills, CA

How to Use This Book

This book is not meant to be read as if it were a typical book. To make it easier to focus on and ponder each message to the fullest, there is only one quote on each page. Flip this book open to a "random" page and see what message appears, for it will be a synchronistic message from the universe. Feel free to leave the book open for the entire day so that you can ponder the message it contains for you (the spiral-bound edition is especially useful for this purpose). Daily use is recommended for the most powerful and sustained effect.

The infinity symbol at the bottom of the pages with quotes will remind you of your true nature as an infinite being living in an infinite cosmos.

"Programming languages are like girlfriends/boyfriends: The new one is better because 'you' are better."

~ Unknown

"Our true wealth
is the good we do
in this world.
None of us has faith
unless we desire
for our neighbors
what we desire for ourselves."

~ Mohammad

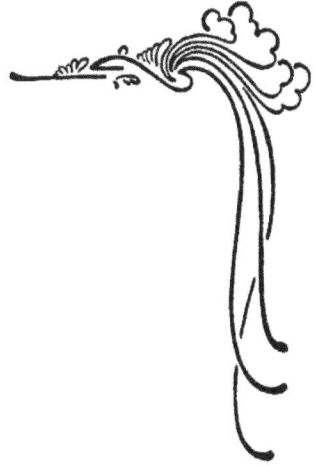

"*Random events
will conspire
to make you happy
if you know
what to look for.*"

~ Unknown

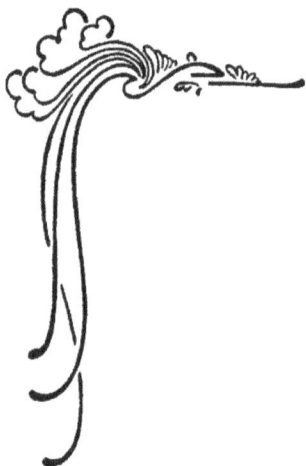

"Rather than praying/asking for something, sometimes it's better to ask 'what is the question?'"

~ Brent N. Hunter

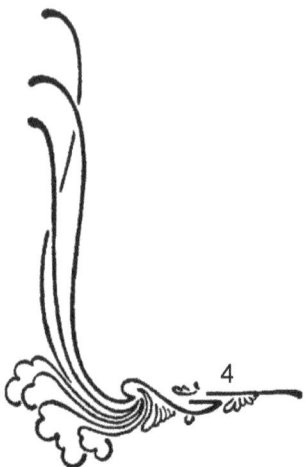

∞

"Read not to contradict
and confute, nor
to find talk and discourse,
but to weigh and consider."

~ Sir Francis Bacon

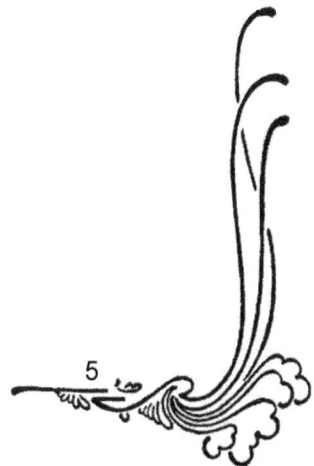

∞

"*Real peace of mind
is the companion
of the silence of the mind.*"

~ Remez Sasson

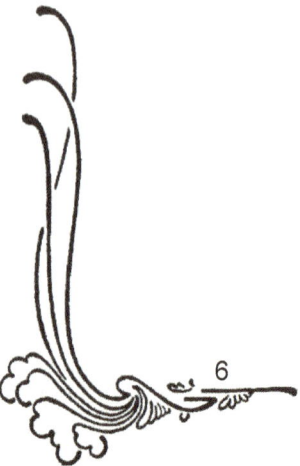

6

"*Reality
is merely an illusion,
albeit a very persistent one.*"

~ Albert Einstein

∞

"*Realize deeply
that the present moment
is all you ever have.*"

~ Eckhart Tolle

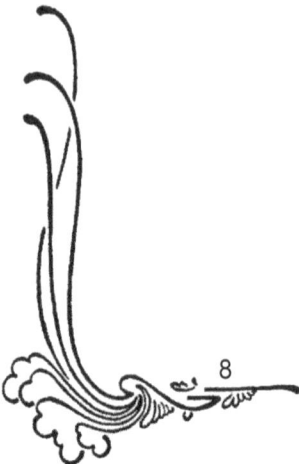

"Realize you are
on a journey
to higher consciousness.
Expand your awareness
through meditation,
contemplation
and other means."

~ Deepak Chopra

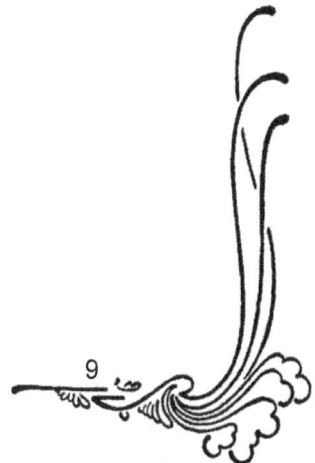

∞

"Remember
that everyone you meet
is afraid of something,
loves something
and has lost something."

~ Jackson Brown

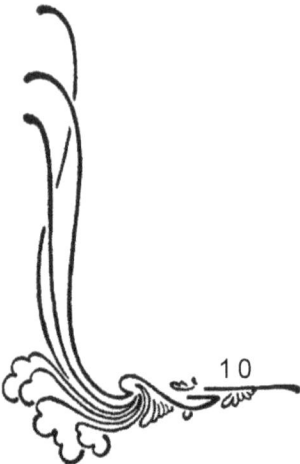

∞

"Remember
that not getting
what you want is sometimes
a wonderful stroke of luck."

~ HH The Dalai Lama

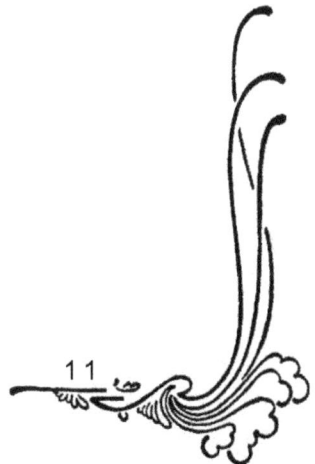

∞

11

"*Responsibility
is the price of freedom.*"

~ Elbert Hubbard

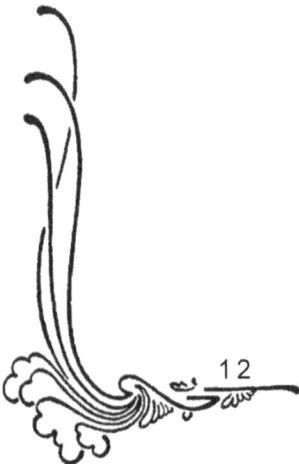

∞

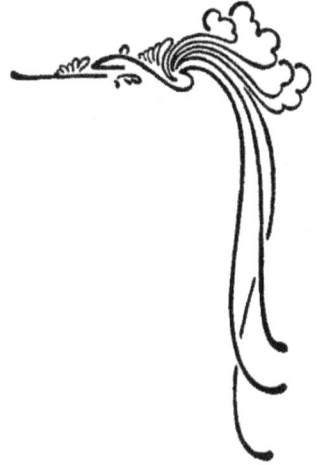

"Right
temporarily defeated,
is stronger
than evil triumphant."

~ Martin Luther King, Jr.

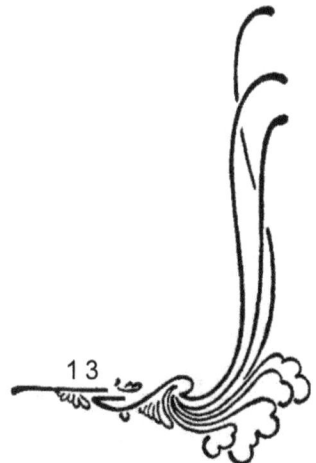

∞

"Row, row, row
your boat...
life is but a dream."

~ Children's nursery rhyme

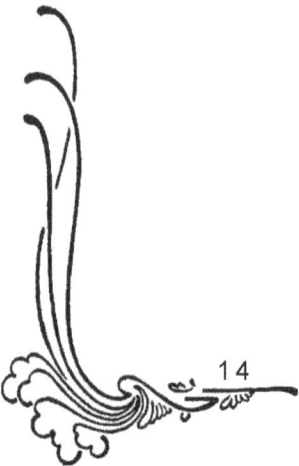

∞

"Safeguarding
the rights of others
is the most noble
and beautiful end
of a human being."

~ Kahlil Gibran

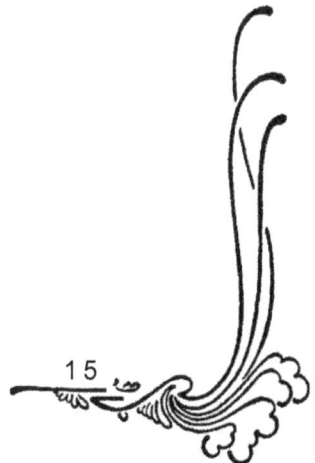

∞

"Be so busy improving yourself that you have no time to criticize others."

~ Chetan Bhagat

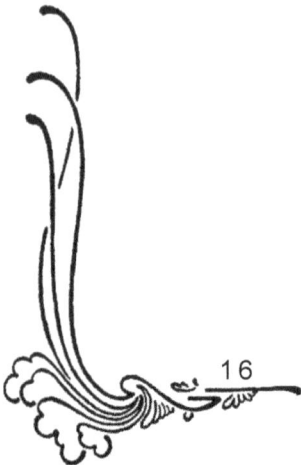

∞

"See yourself doing
the things you'll be doing
when you've reached
your goal."

~ Earl Nightingale

∞

"Seek first to understand, then to be understood."

~ Stephen Covey

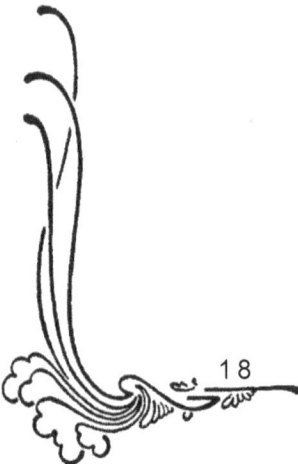

"Self-realization is effortless.
What you are trying to find
is what you already are."

~ Ramesh Balsekar

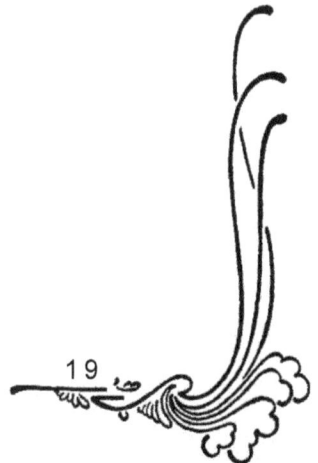

∞

"It is no measure of health to be well adjusted to a profoundly sick society."

~ Jiddu Krishnamurti

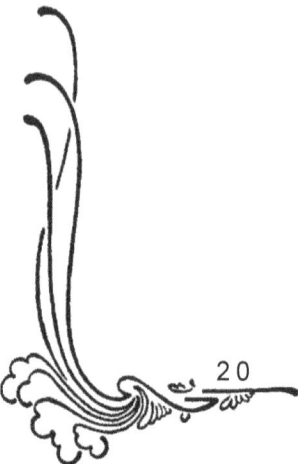

∞

"The way
to develop decisiveness
is to start right
where you are,
with the very next question
you face."

~ Napoleon Hill

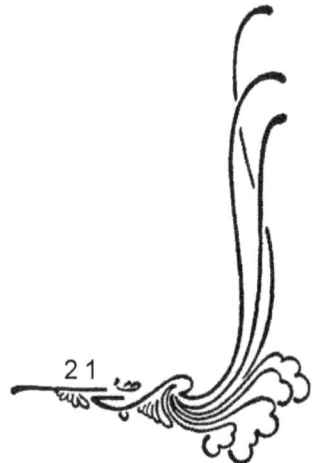

"Set peace of mind
as your highest goal,
and organize
your life around it."

~ Brian Tracy

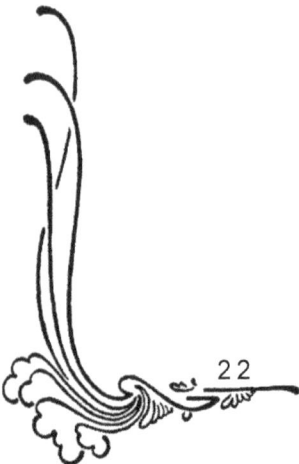

"Slow down and enjoy life. It's not only the scenery you miss by going too fast, you also miss the sense of where you are going and why."

~ Eddie Cantor

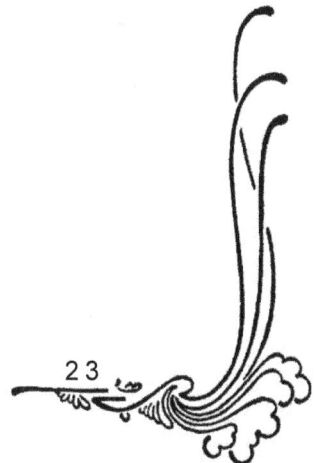

"The best and most beautiful things in the world cannot be seen or even touched – they must be felt with the heart."

~ Helen Keller

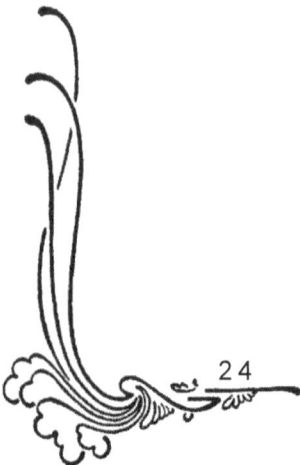

24

"Intelligence
is the ability
to adapt to change."

~ Stephen Hawking

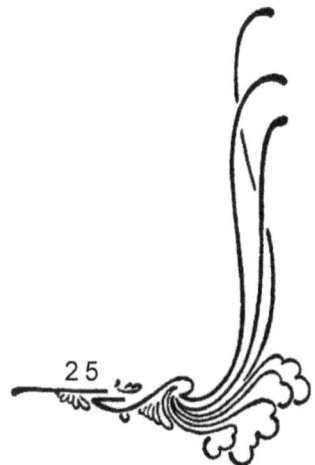

∞

"Some people
are waiting for
Martin Luther King, Jr.
or Mahatma Gandhi
to come back —
but they are gone.
It is up to us."

~ Marian Wright Edelman

∞

"Some men have
thousands of reasons
why they cannot do
what they want to,
when all they need
is one reason why they can.

~ Willis R. Whitney

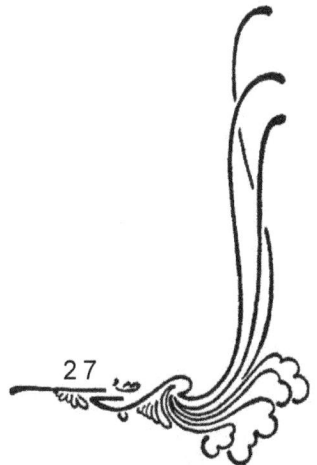

"Some things have to be believed to be seen."

~ Ralph Hodgson

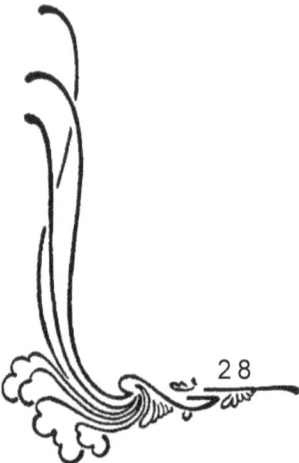

∞

"*He who knows best knows how little he knows.*"

~ Thomas Jefferson

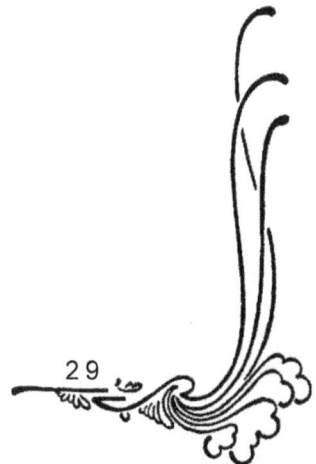

∞

"Sometimes,
it's not about
praying for guidance,
clarity or things.
Sometimes, it's more helpful
to ask 'what is the question?'"

~ Brent N. Hunter

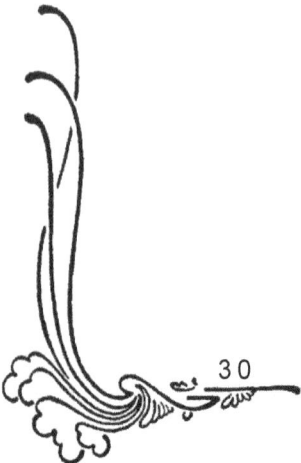

∞

*"You do not attract
what you want,
you attract what you are."*

~ Wayne Dyer

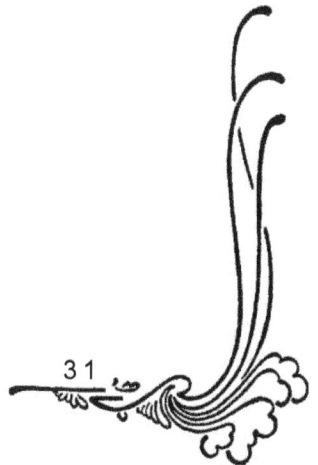

31

"Sometimes
the most important thing
in a whole day
is the rest we take
between two deep breaths."

~ Etty Hillesum

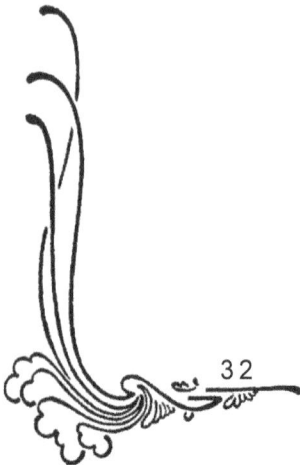

∞

"Sometimes
your joy is the source
of your smile,
but sometimes your smile
can be the source
of your joy."

~ Thich Nhât Hanh

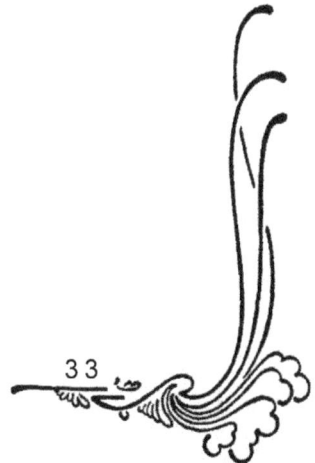

∞

"Sometimes,
your only available
transportation is a leap
of faith."

~ Margaret Shepherd

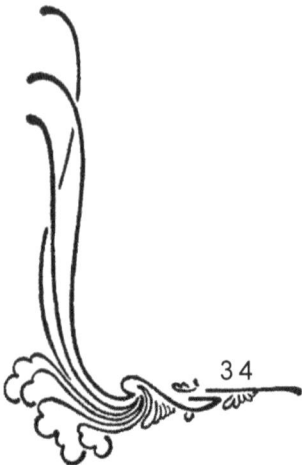

"Sometimes,
we need to go
to the opposite side
of the world
to realize assumptions
that we didn't know we had
and realize the opposite
may also be true."

~ Derek Sivers

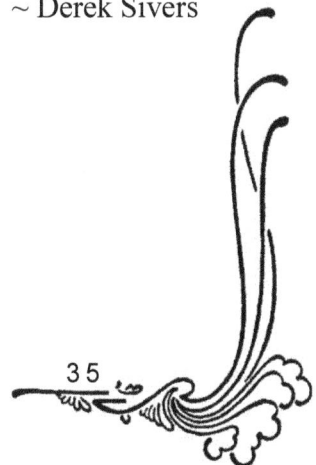

"Start by doing
what's necessary;
then do what's possible;
suddenly, you are doing
the impossible."

~ St. Francis of Assisi

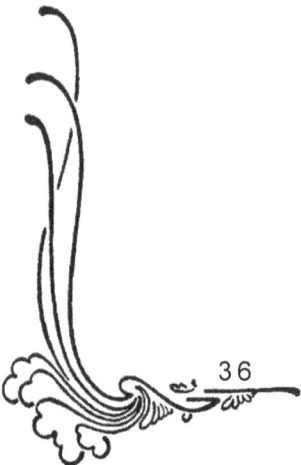

∞

"*Stop at Nothing to Start Something.*"

~ Quote on sign in Los Angeles restaurant

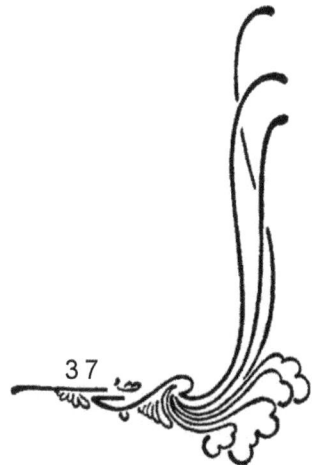

∞

37

"Strength doesn't come
from physical capacity.
It comes from
an indomitable will."

~ Mahatma Gandhi

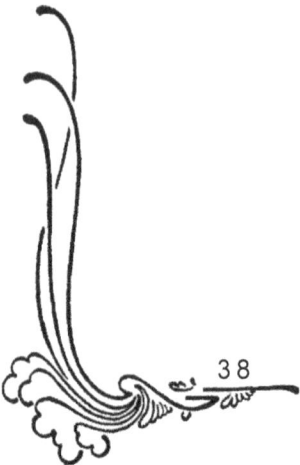

"Stumbling
is not falling."

~ Portuguese Proverb

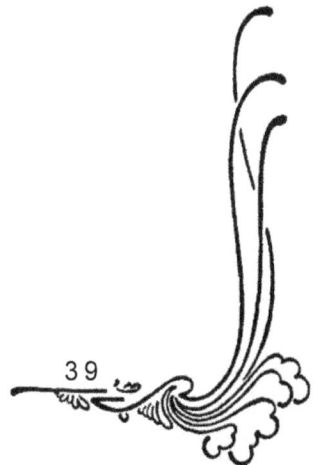

∞

"*Success comes in cans,
failure in can'ts.*"

~ Wilfred Peterson

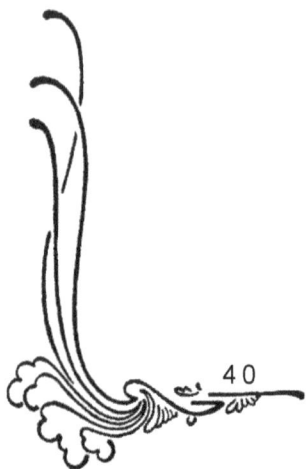

"Success is how high you bounce after you hit bottom."

~ General George S. Patton

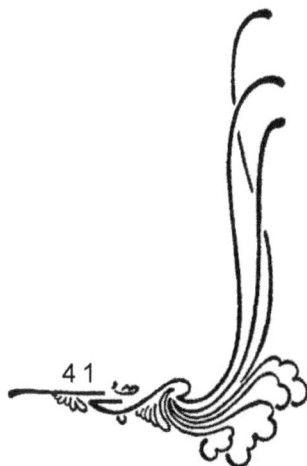

"Success is one percent
of inspiration
and ninety-nine percent
of perspiration."

~ Thomas Edison

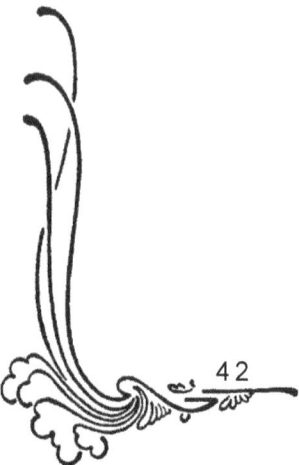

∞

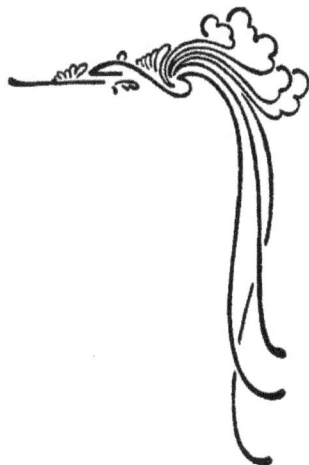

"Success
is the ability to fulfill
your desires
with effortless ease."

~ Deepak Chopra

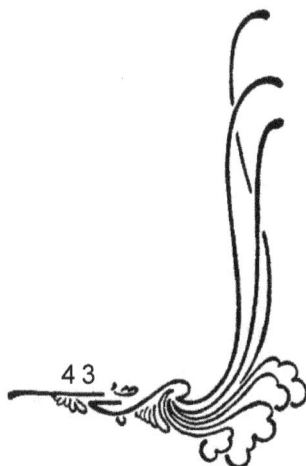

"Success
isn't the key to happiness,
happiness is the key

to success.

If you love
what you are doing,
you will be successful."

~ Albert Schweitzer

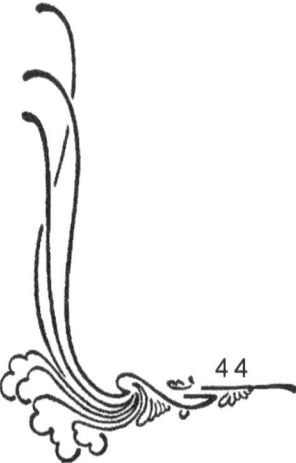

∞

"*Support and encouragement
are like vitamins
for the soul.*"

~ Dr. Tom V. Morris

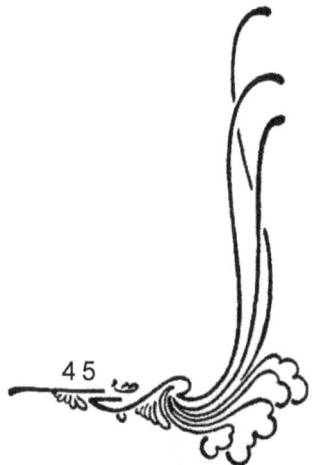

∞

45

"Surround yourself
with only people
who are going
to lift you higher."

~ Oprah Winfrey

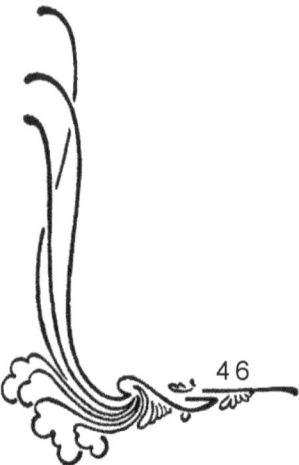

∞

"*Surround yourself
with people who believe
in you.*"

~ Brian Koslow

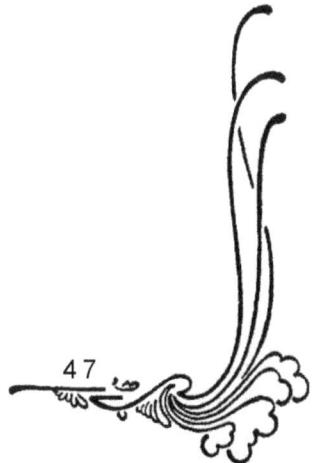

"*Tact is the ability
to describe others
as they see themselves.*"

~ Abraham Lincoln

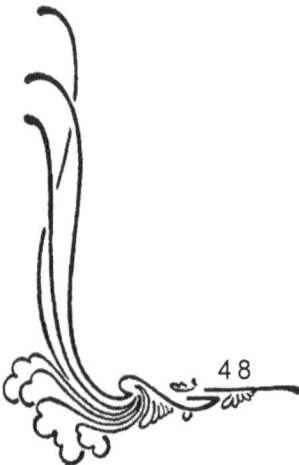

∞

"Take heed
you do not find
what you do not seek."

~ English Proverb

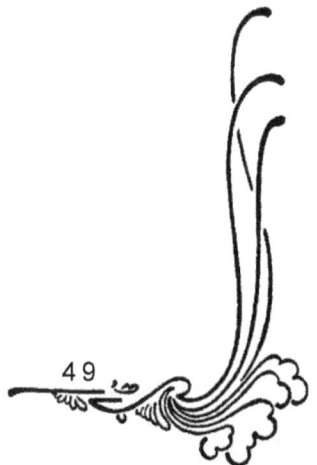

∞

*"TEAM —
Together
Everyone Achieves More."*

~ Unknown

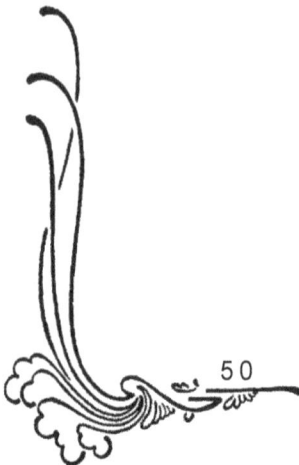

*"Teamwork divides the task
and doubles the success."*

~ Unknown

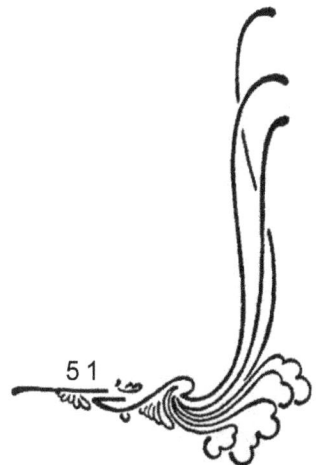

"Teamwork:
Simply stated,
it is less me and more we."

~ Unknown

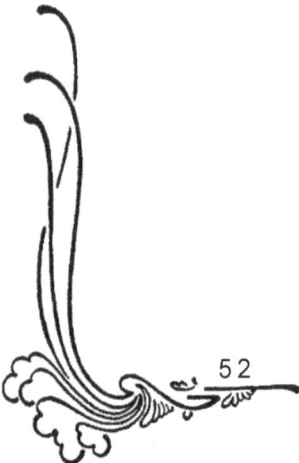

"Tell me and I forget;
show me and I remember;
involve me
and I understand."

~ Anonymous

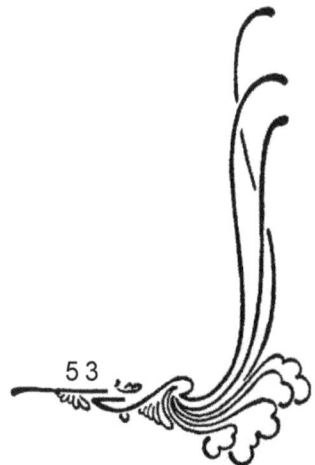

*"Tell me,
what is it you plan to do
with your one wild
and precious life?"*

~ Mary Oliver

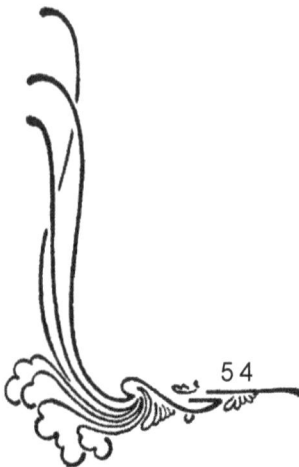

"That which does not kill us
makes us stronger.
Nietzsche Restated:
everything either empowers
or disempowers us;
the choice is ours."

~ Unknown

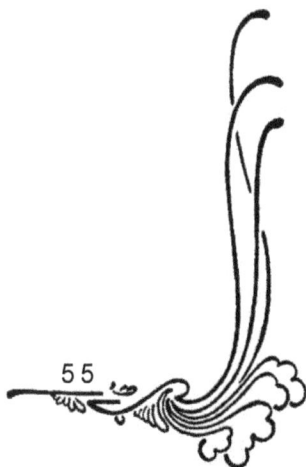

"The ancestor of every action
is a thought."

~ Ralph Waldo Emerson

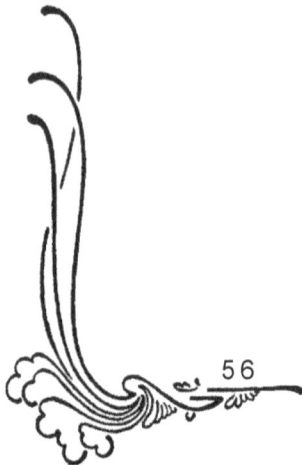

"The art of being wise
is knowing what to overlook."

~ William James

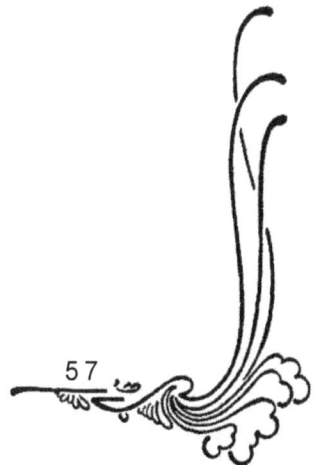

"The best
and most beautiful things
in the world cannot be seen,
nor touched...but are felt
in the heart."

~ Helen Keller

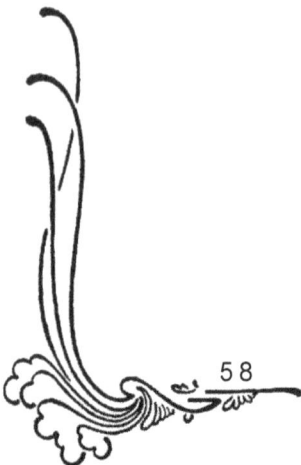

"The best love
is the kind
that awakens the soul
and makes us reach for more,
that plants a fire
in our hearts
and brings peace
to our minds."

~ Nicholas Sparks

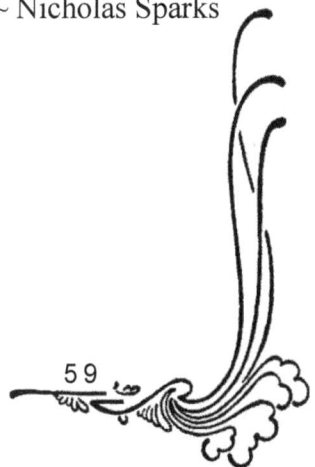

∞

"The best thing
about the future
is that it comes
only one day at a time."

~ Abraham Lincoln

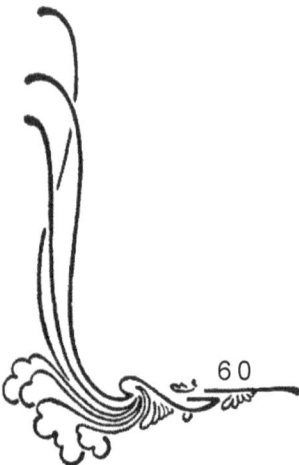

∞

"The best vision
is insight."

~ Malcolm Forbes

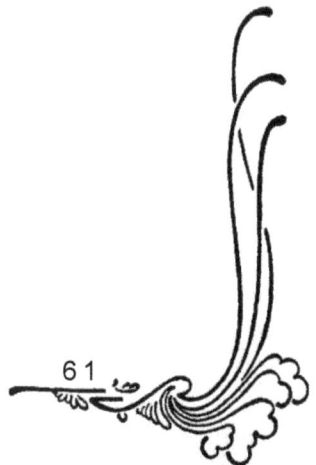

∞

"The best way
to cheer yourself up
is to try to cheer
someone else up."

~ Mark Twain

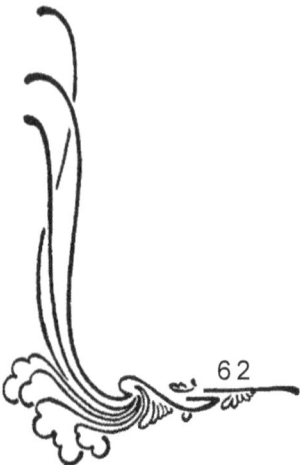

"The best way
to predict the future
is to create it."

~ Peter Drucker

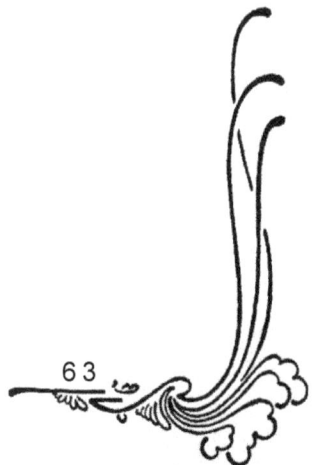

∞

"The bird of paradise
alights only upon the hand
that does not grasp."

~ John Berry

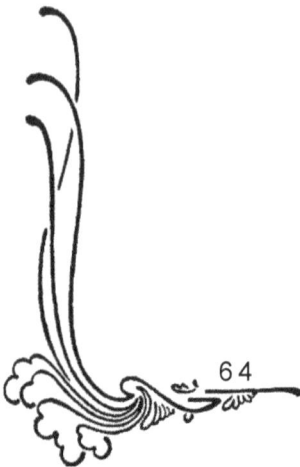

"The block of granite
which was an obstacle
on the path of the weak
becomes a stepping stone
in the path of the strong."

~ Thomas Carlyle

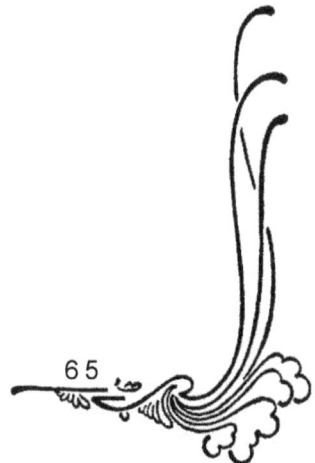

∞

65

"The bravest sight
in the world is to see
a great man struggling
against adversity."

~ Seneca

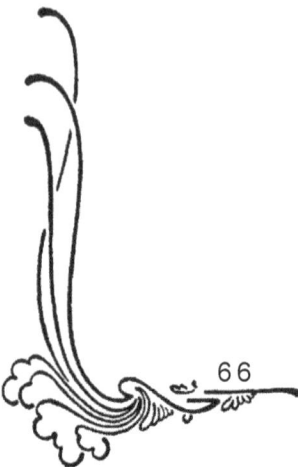

66

"The care
of human life and happiness,
and not their destruction,
is the first and only object
of good government."

~ Thomas Jefferson

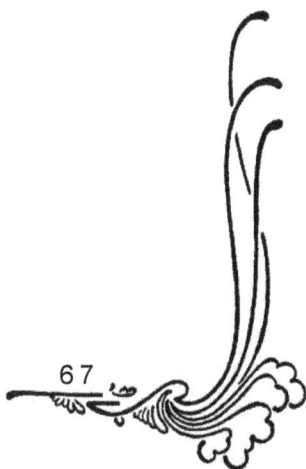

∞

"The clearest way
into the universe
is through a forest wilderness."

~ John Muir

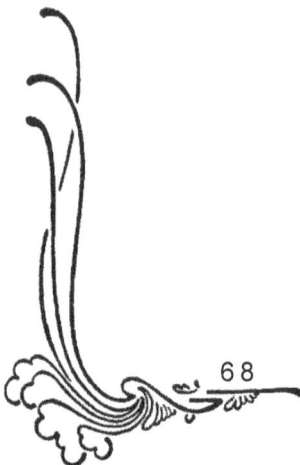

"The Constitution
is not neutral.
It was designed to take
the government off the backs
of people."

~ Justice William O. Douglas

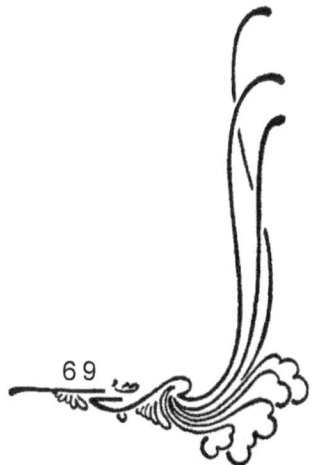

"The cyclone derives its powers
from a calm center.
So does a person."

~ Norman Vincent Peale

∞

"The day will come
when all God's children
from bass black
to treble white
will be significant
on the constitution's
keyboard."

~ Martin Luther King, Jr.

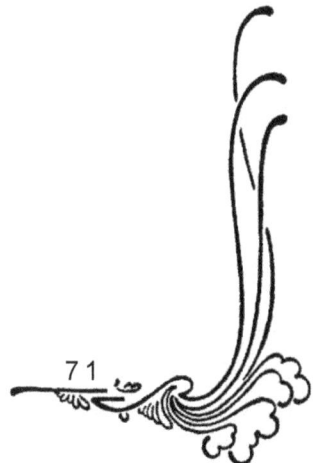

∞

71

"The day,
water, sun, moon, night —
I do not have to purchase
these things with money."

~ Plautus

"The difference
between a stumbling block
and a stepping stone
is how you use them."

~ Unknown

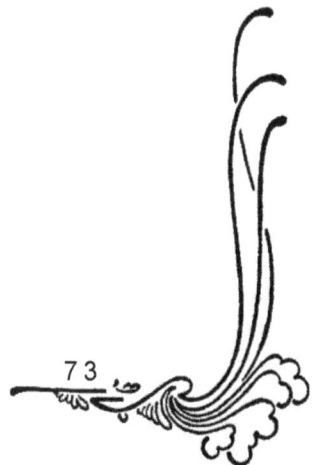

"The difference between
try and triumph
is a little umph."

~ Unknown

"The first
and the best victory
is to conquer self."

~ Plato

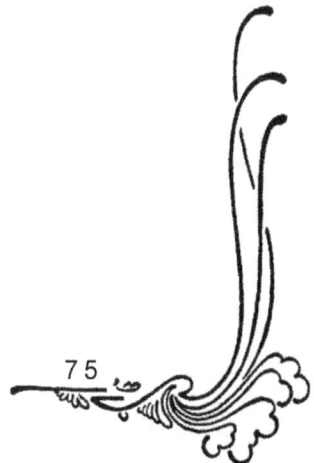

"The first principal
of nonviolent action
is that of non-cooperation
with everything humiliating."

~ César Chávez

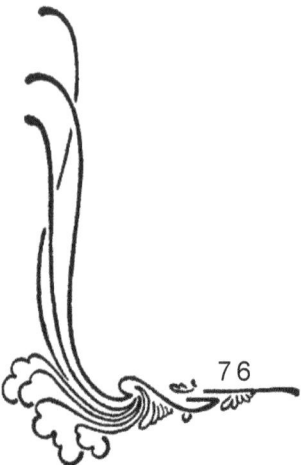

"The first wealth
is health."

~ Ralph Waldo Emerson

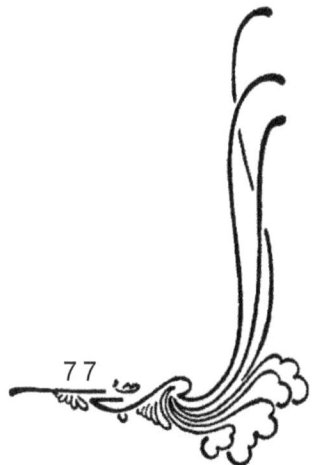

∞

"The fragrance
always remains on the hand
that gives the rose."

~ Unknown

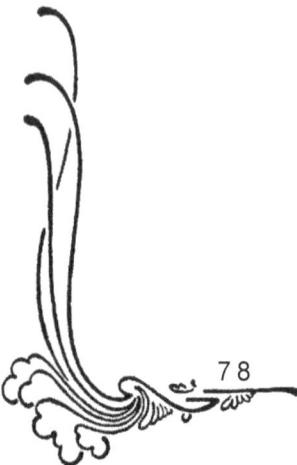

78

"The future belongs
to those who believe
in the beauty
of their dreams."

~ Eleanor Roosevelt

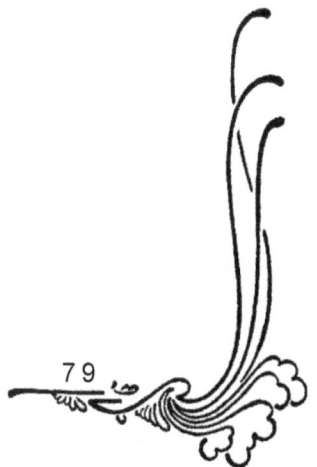

"The great thing
about getting older
is that you don't lose
all the other ages you've been."

~ Madeleine L'Engle

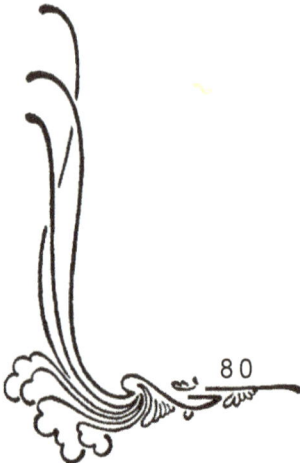

"The greatest discovery
of all time is that a person
can change his future
by merely changing
his attitude."

~ Oprah Winfrey

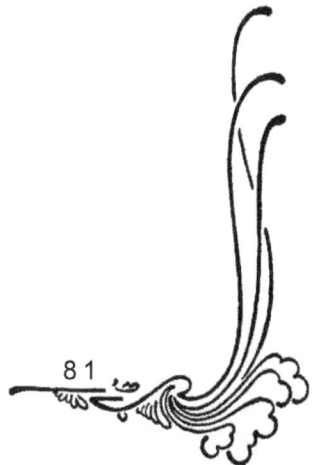

∞

"Everything in the universe
is within you.
Ask all from yourself."

~ Jalāl ad-Dīn Muhammad Balkhī "Rumi"

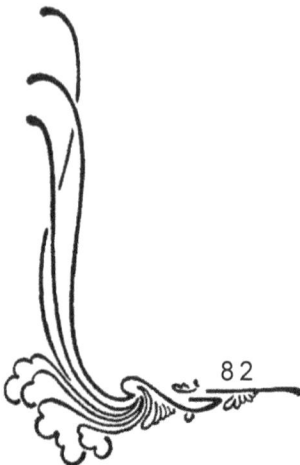

"The greatest flaw
of human nature
is that we can eventually
take even paradise
for granted."

~ Unknown

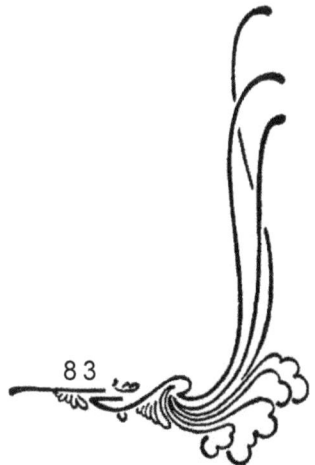

"The greatest glory in living
lies not in never falling,
but in rising
every time we fall."

~ Nelson Mandela

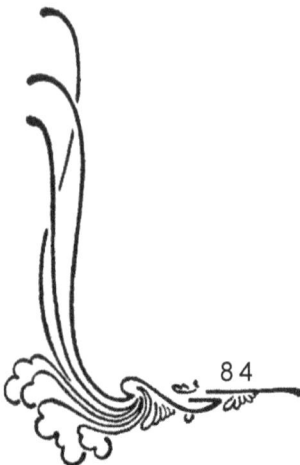

"The heart is
the hub of all sacred places.
Go there and roam in it."

~ Bhagawan Nityananda

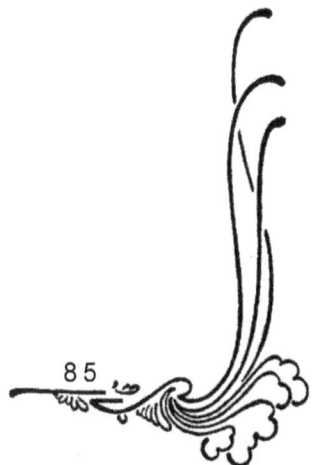

"The heart
is the shining light
of our being — allow it
to brighten your day
and all whom you meet."

~ Unknown

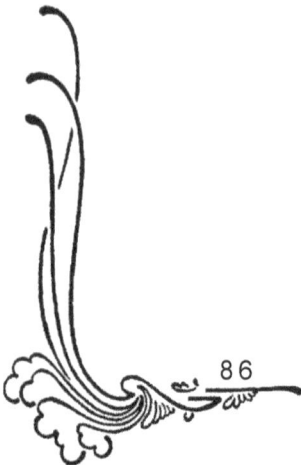

"The height
of your accomplishments
will equal the depth
of your convictions."

~ William F. Scolavino

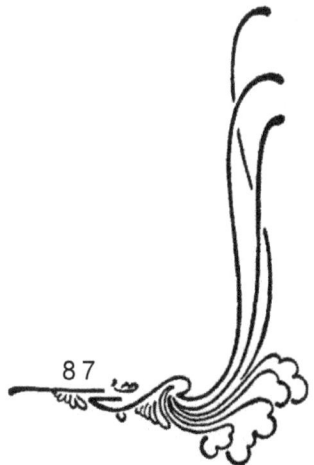

∞

"The highest form
of ignorance
is to reject something
you know nothing about."

~ Wayne Dyer

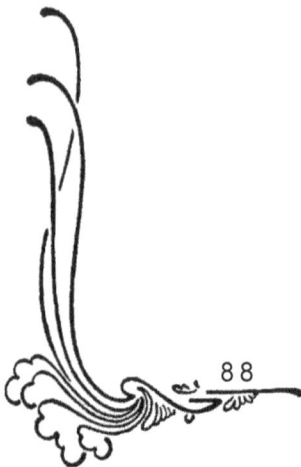

88

"The human mind
will not be confined
to any limits."

~ Johann Wolfgang Von Goethe

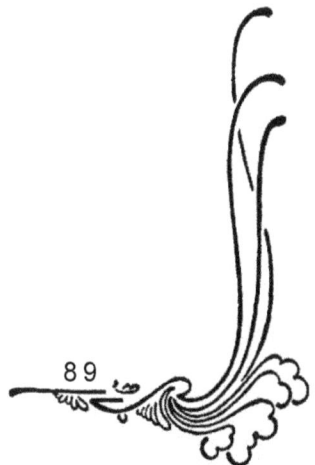

∞

"The inability
of those in power
to still the voices
of their own consciences
is the great force
leading to change."

~ Kenneth Kaunda

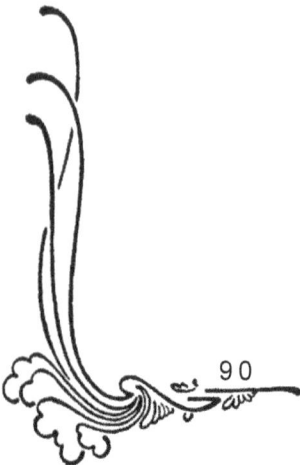

∞

"The infinite consciousness
is nameless and formless,
but names and forms
are associated
to its reflections."

~ Deepak Chopra

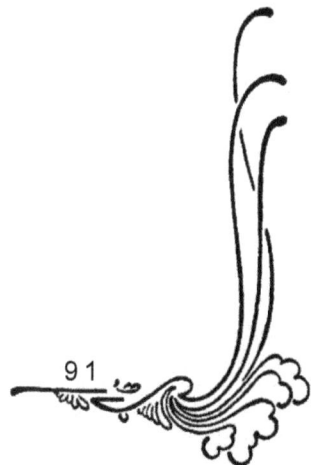

∞

"The leaders of mankind
are those who lift their feet
from the dusty road
and lift their eyes
to the illumined future."

~ Woodrow Wilson

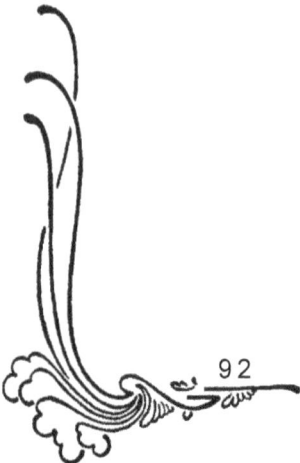

∞

"The least I can do
is speak out for those
who cannot speak
for themselves."

~ Jane Goodall

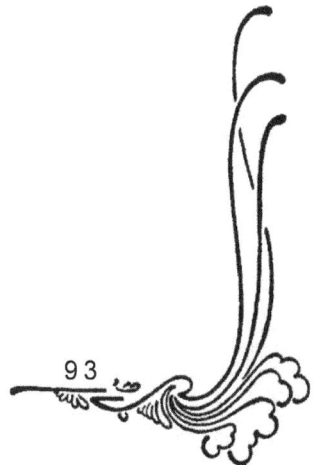

"The little unremembered
acts of kindness and love
are the best parts
of a person's life."

~ William Wordsworth

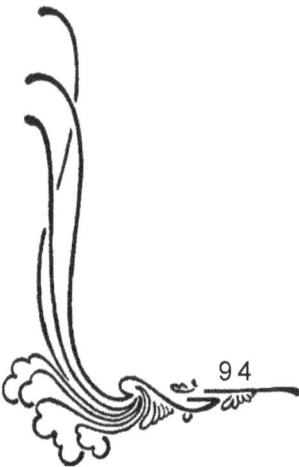

"The meeting
of two personalities
is like the contact
of two chemical substances:
if there is any reaction,
both are transformed."

~ C.G. Jung

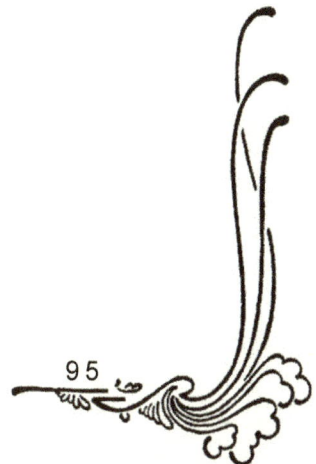

"If you can't feed
a hundred people,
then feed just one."

~ Mother Teresa

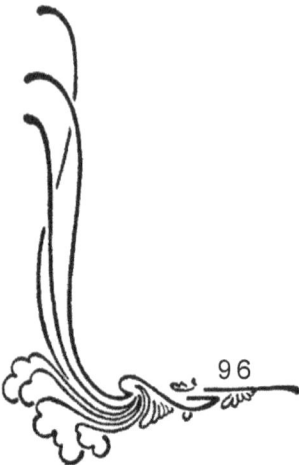

∞

"The mind
is its own place, and in itself,
can make heaven of Hell,
and a hell of Heaven."

~ John Milton

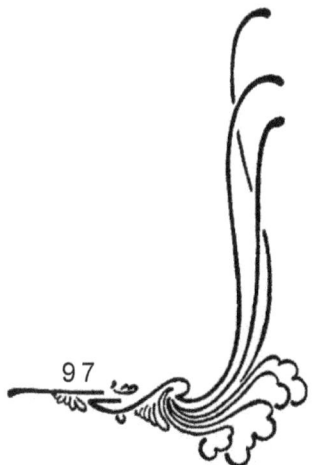

"The mind
is not a vessel to be filled,
but a fire to be kindled."

~ Plutarch

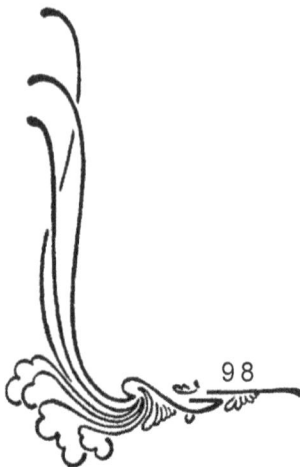

"The mind of the bigot
is like the pupil of the eye:
the more light you pour on it
the more it will contract."

~ Oliver Wendell Holmes

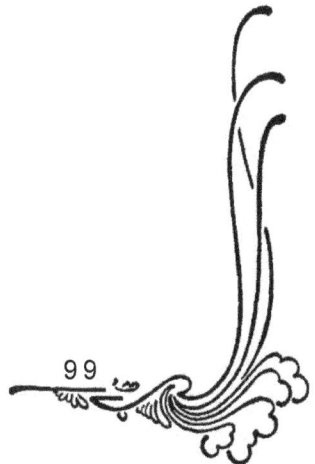

∞

"The moral law
commands us to make
the highest possible good
in a world
the final object
of all our conduct."

~ Paul Ricoeur

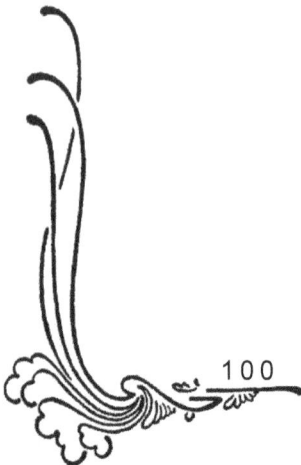

100

"The more freedom we enjoy,
the greater the responsibility
we bear toward others,
as well as ourselves."

~ Óscar Arias Sánchez

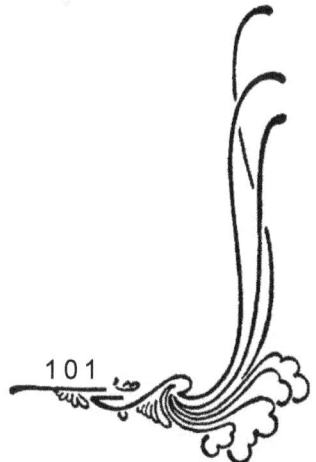

∞

"The more you praise
and celebrate your life,
the more there is in life
to celebrate."

~ Oprah Winfrey

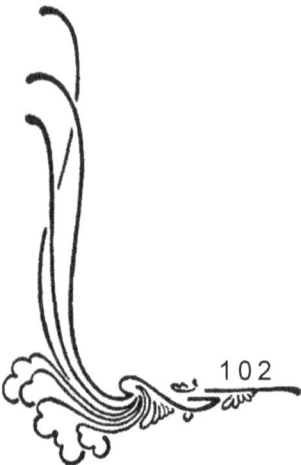

"The more you want
to get something done,
the less it's called work."

~ Richard Bach

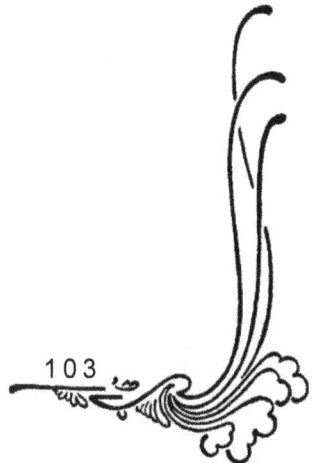

"The most difficult battles
we fight are the battles
within ourselves.
Focus within."

~ Brent N. Hunter

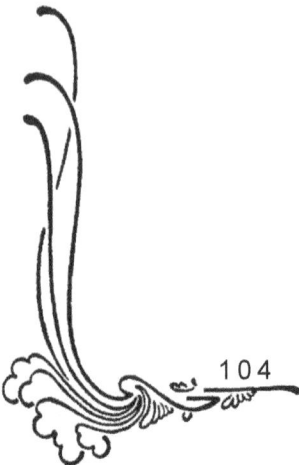

"The mountain
to the climber
is clearer from the plain."

~ Kahlil Gibran

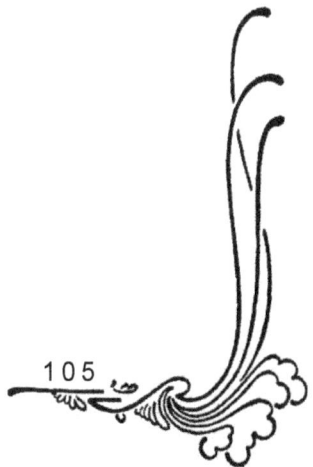

∞

"The need
to feel and express love
and compassion for everyone,
knowing that we are all
part of a greater reality
is the core of all spirituality."

~ Mātā Amṛtānandamayī Devī "Amma"

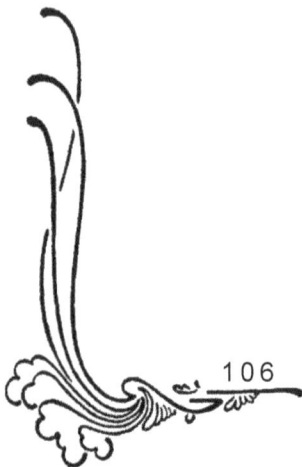

"The nice thing about egotists
is that they don't talk
about other people."

~ Lucille S. Harper

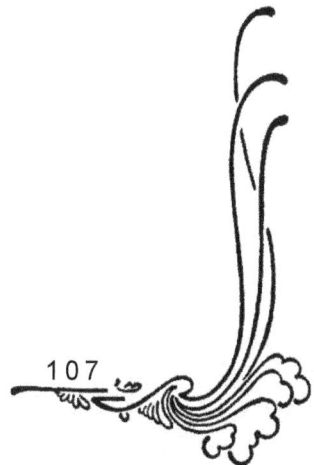

∞

"The nice thing
about teamwork is that
you always have others
on your side."

~ Margaret Carty

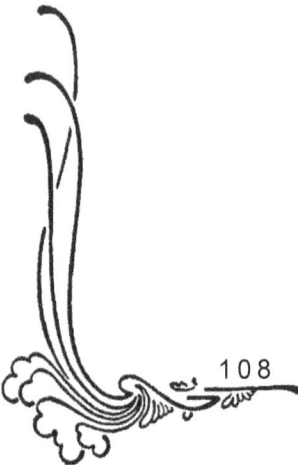

"The only reason for time
is so that everything
doesn't happen at once."

~ Albert Einstein

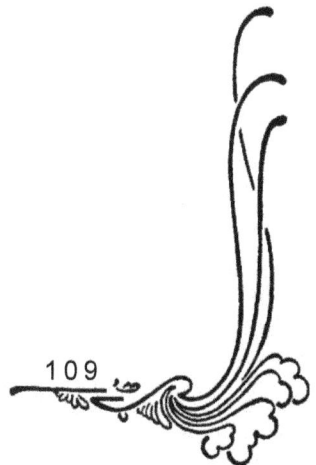

∞

"The only thing necessary
for the triumph of evil
is for good men
to do nothing."

~ Edmund Burke

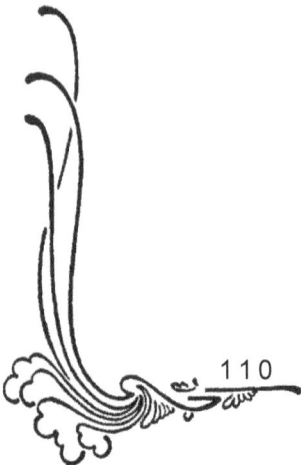

"The only way
of finding the limits
of the possible is by
going beyond them
into the impossible."

~ Arthur C. Clarke

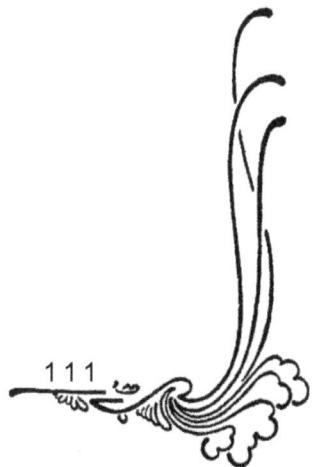

∞

"The only way
to have a friend
is to be one."

~ Ralph Waldo Emerson

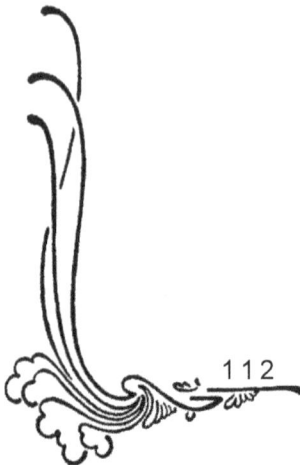

"The opposite of love
isn't hate,
it's indifference."

~ Elie Wiesel

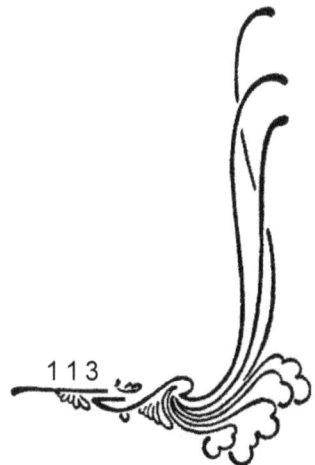

"The path to greatness
is along with others."

~ Baltasar Gracián y Morales

∞

"The person who says
it cannot be done
should not interrupt
the person doing it."

~ Chinese Proverb

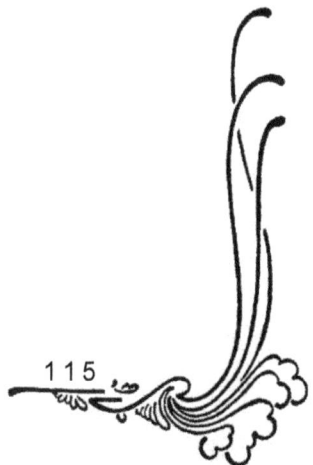

"The pessimist
sees difficulty
in every opportunity.
The optimist
sees the opportunity
in every difficulty."

~ Sir Winston Churchill

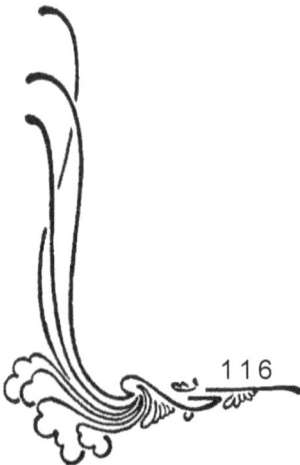

∞

"The Positive Thinker
Sees the Invisible...
Feels the Intangible...
and Achieves
the Impossible."

~ Mallika Chopra

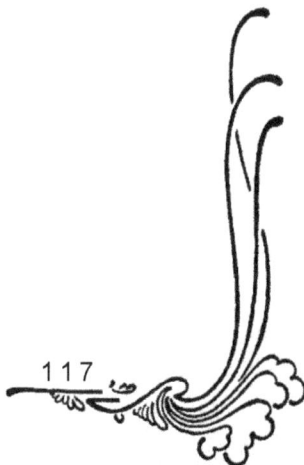

∞

"The power
of choosing good and evil
is within the reach of all."

~ Origen Adamantius

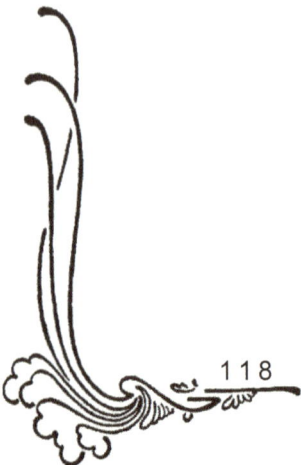

∞

"The power of imagination makes us infinite."

~ John Muir

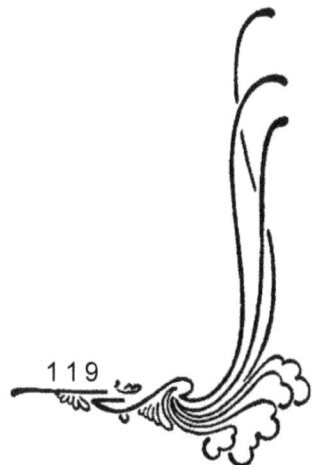

"It is during our darkest moments that we must focus to see the light."

~ Aristotle Onassis

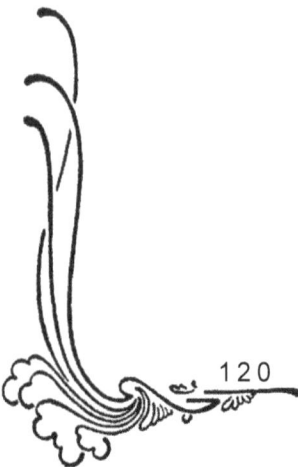

"The purpose of life
is a life of purpose."

~ Robert Byrne

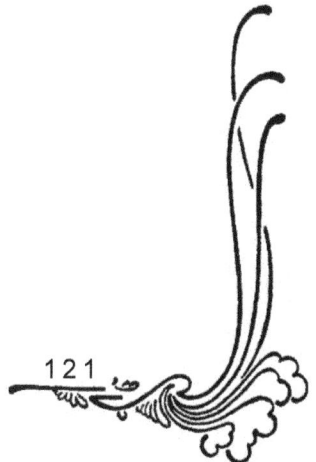

"The race does not always go
to the swift,
but to those
who keep on running."

~ Unknown

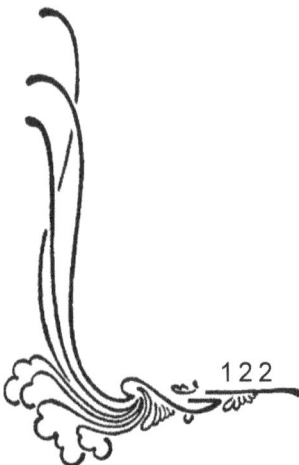

"The real voyage of discovery
consists not in seeking
new lands, but in seeing
with new eyes."

~ Marcel Proust

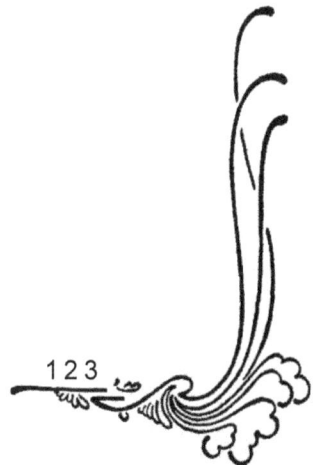

∞

123

"The secret of getting ahead
is getting started."

~ Mark Twain

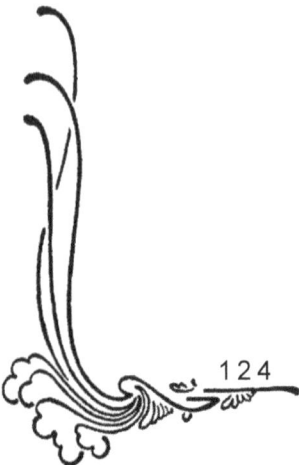

"*The secret of happiness is to make others believe they are the cause of it.*"

~ Al Batt

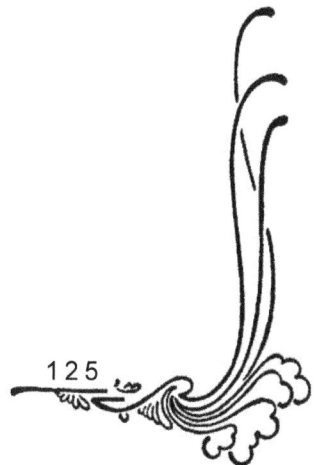

"The secret of success
is to do common things
uncommonly well."

~ John D. Rockefeller, Sr.

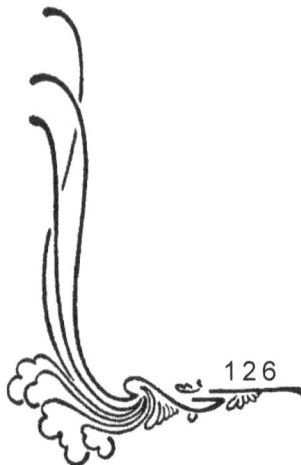

∞

"The sunshine
is always shining
above the clouds."

~ Brent N. Hunter

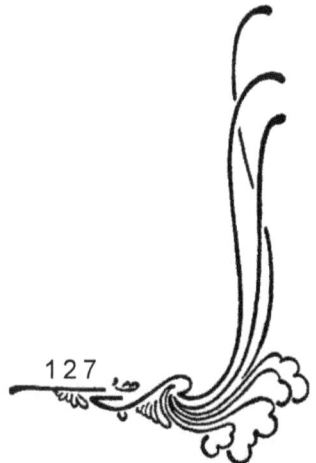

∞

"The test of the morality
of a society
is what it does
for its children."

~ Dietrich Bonhoeffer

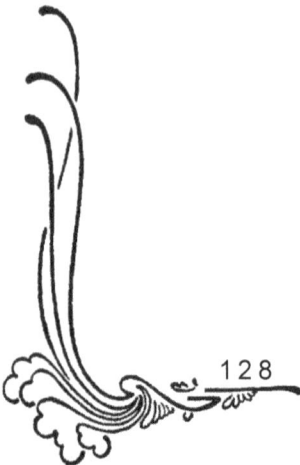

∞

"The thing always happens
that you really believe in;
and the belief in a thing
makes it happen."

~ Frank Lloyd Wright

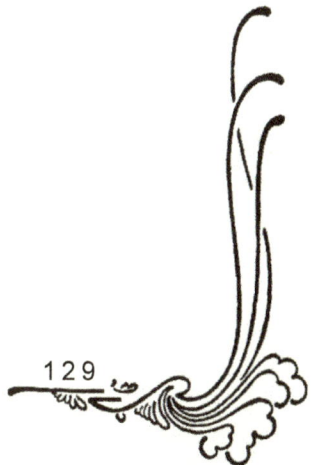

"The thing
that is really hard
and really amazing
is giving up on being perfect
and beginning the work
of becoming yourself."

~ Anna Quindlen

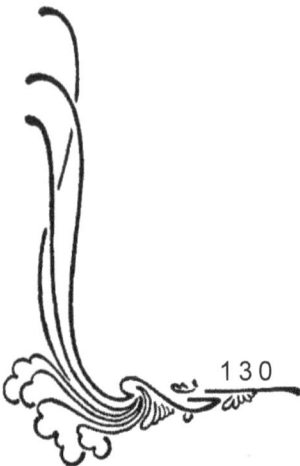

∞

"The things
that one most wants to do
are the things that are
probably most worth doing."

~ Winifred Holtby

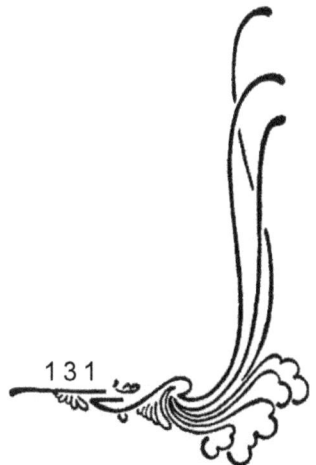

∞

"The thoughts
we choose to think
are the tools we use
to paint the canvas
of our lives."

~ Louise L. Hay

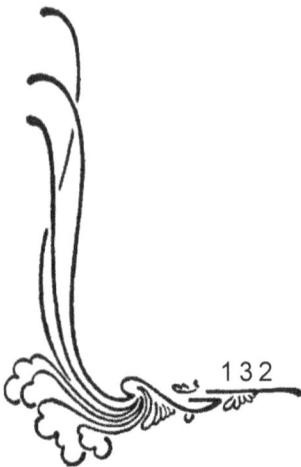

"The thoughts
you think today
are the predictors of
the results you'll see
tomorrow."

~ Unknown

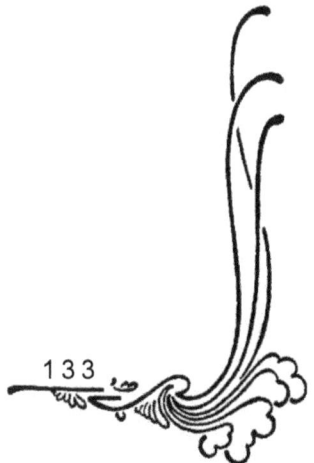

"The time is always right
to do what is right."

~ Martin Luther King, Jr.

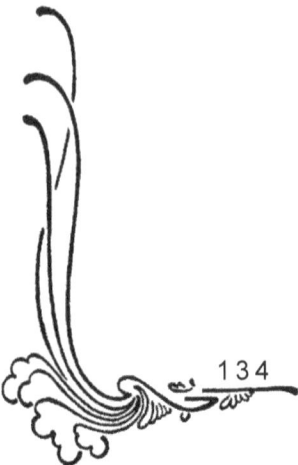

"The trouble with the world
is that the stupid
are cocksure
and the intelligent
are full of doubt."

~ Bertrand Russell

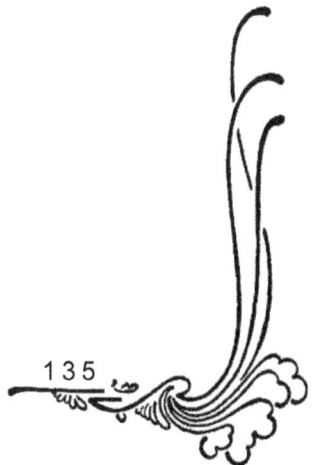

∞

"The true civilization
is where every man gives
to every other every right
that he claims for himself."

~ Robert Ingersoll

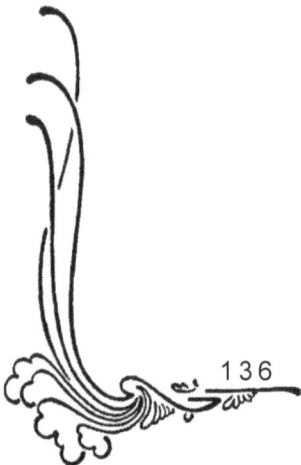

∞

"The truest greatness
lies in being kind,
the truest wisdom
in a happy mind."

~ Ella Wheeler Wilcox

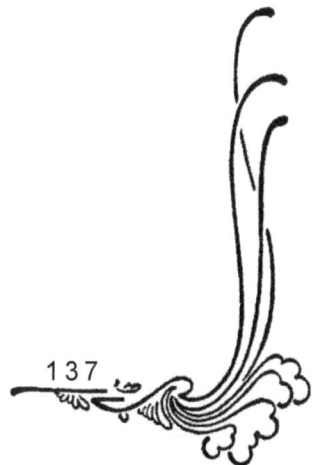

∞

"The universe is full
of magical things
patiently waiting for our wits
to grow sharper."

~ Eden Phillips

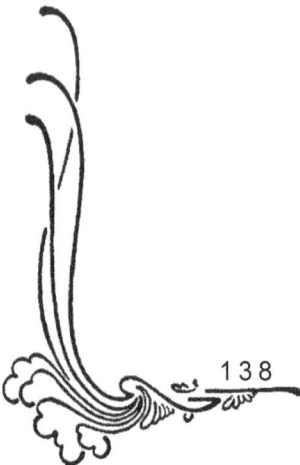

∞

"The way to love anything
is to realize
that it may be lost."

~ G.K. Chesterton

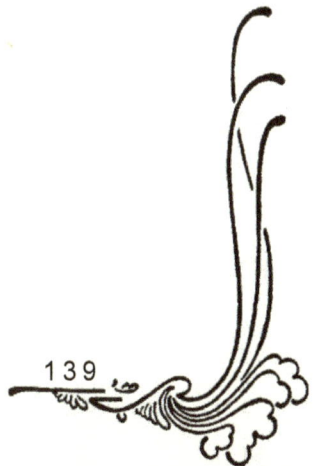

∞

"The way you treat yourself
sets the standard for others."

~ Sonya Friedman

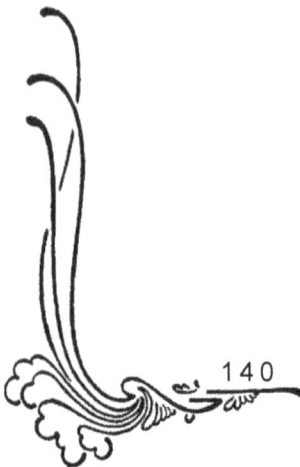

∞

"The whole is greater
than the sum of the parts."

~ Unknown

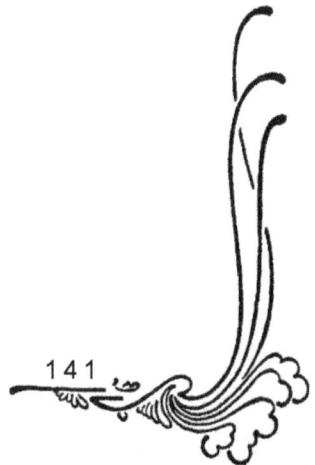

"The wisdom of nature
speaks to the heart,
and nature's first language
is beauty."

~ Tim McNulty

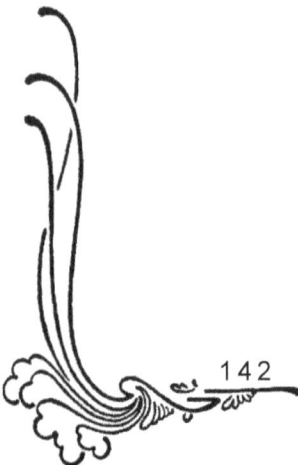

142

"The words of kindness
are more healing
to a drooping heart
than balm or honey."

~ Sarah Fielding

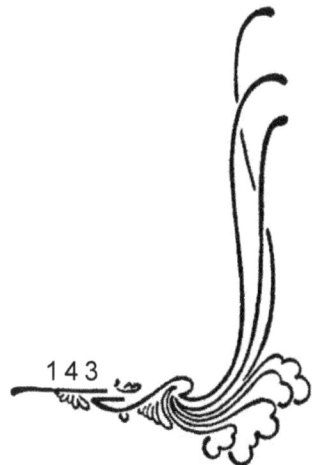

"The world
is a dangerous place,
not because of those
who do evil, but by those
who look on
and do nothing."

~ Albert Einstein

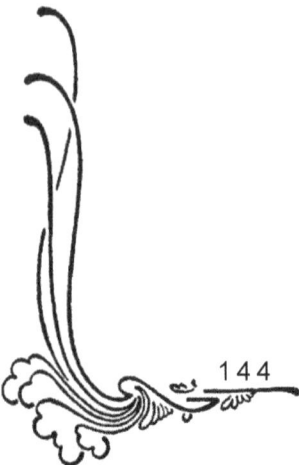

∞

"The world
is hugged by
the faithful arms
of volunteers."

~ Terri Guillemets

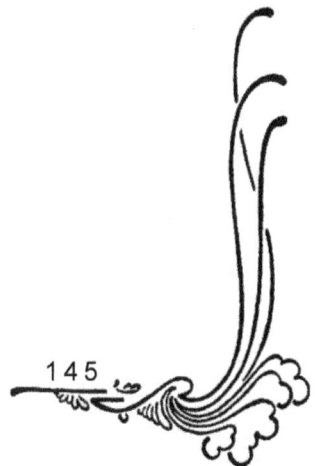

∞

"The world stands aside
to let anyone pass
who knows where he is going."

~ David Starr Jordan

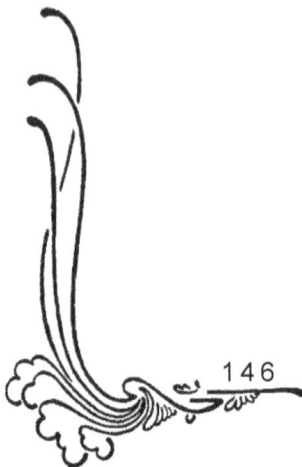

"The young
don't know enough
to be prudent
and therefore they attempt
the impossible and achieve it,
generation after generation."

~ Pearl S. Buck

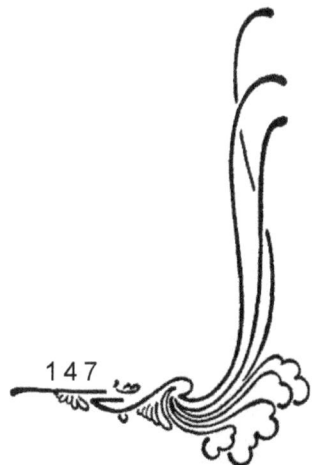

"There are always difficulties
arising that tempt you
to believe your critics
are right."

~ Ralph Waldo Emerson

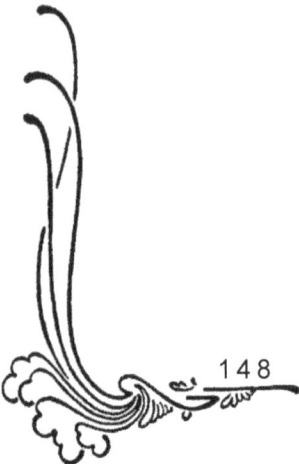

∞

"There are no facts,
only interpretations."

~ Friedrich Nietzsche

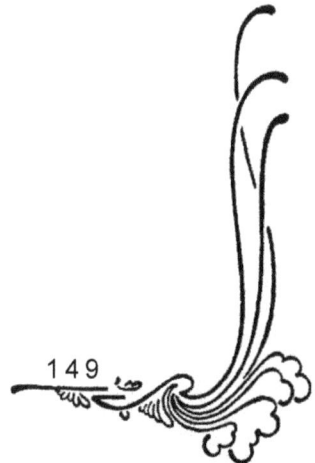

∞

"There are no limitations to the mind except those we acknowledge."

~ Napoleon Hill

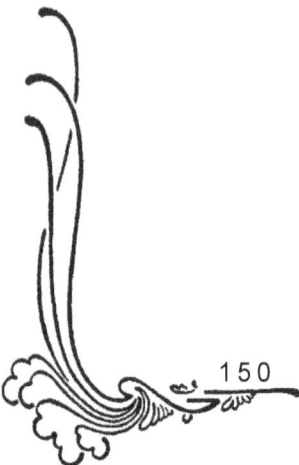

∞

"There are no traffic jams
when you go the extra mile."

~ Anonymous

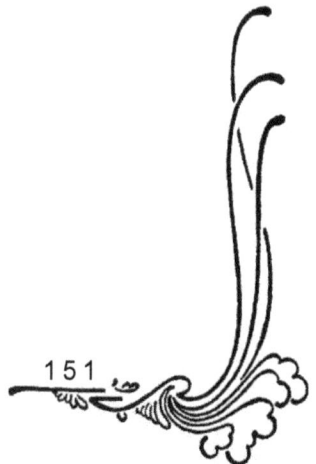

"There are no
unimportant acts of kindness."

~ Anonymous

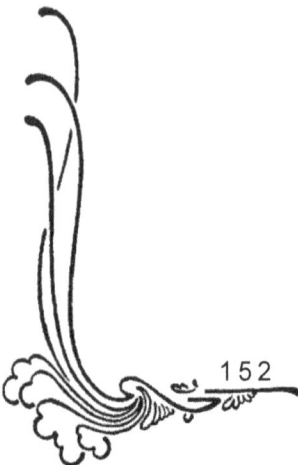

"There are only two mistakes
one can make
along the road to truth;
not going all the way,
and not starting."

~ Buddha

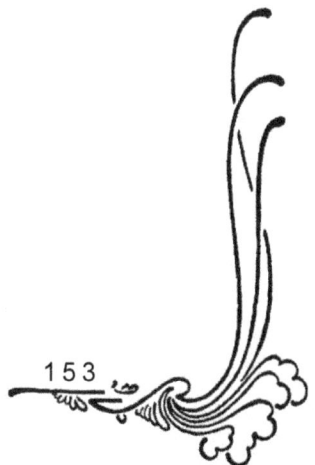

"There are two ways
of spreading light:
to be the candle
or the mirror that reflects it."

~ Edith Wharton

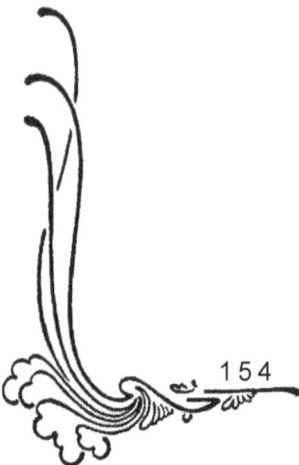

"There came a time
when the risk
to remain tight in the bud
was more painful
than the risk it took
to blossom."

~ Anaïs Nin

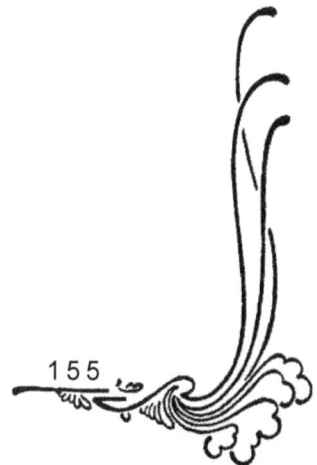

"There can be no
daily democracy
without daily citizenship."

~ Ralph Nader

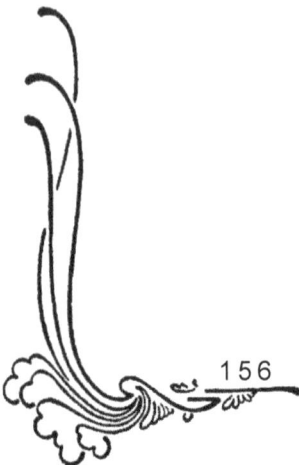

"There is one thing
we do know: that we are here
for the sake of each other."

~ Albert Einstein

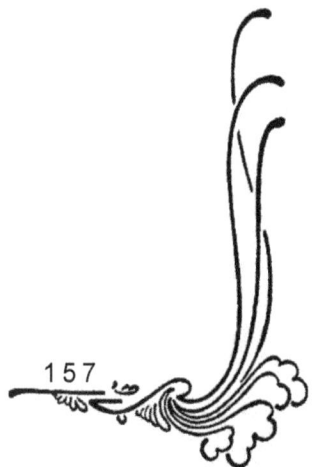

∞

"There is no such thing
as a little freedom —
either you are all free
or you are not free."

~ Walter Cronkite

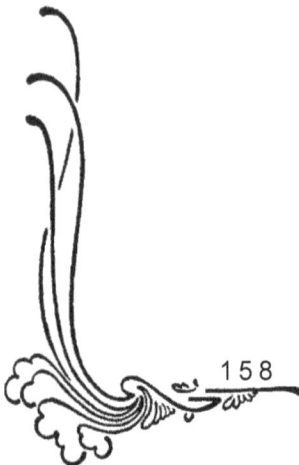

"Don't judge each day by the harvest you reap, but by the seeds that you plant."

~ Robert Louis Stevenson

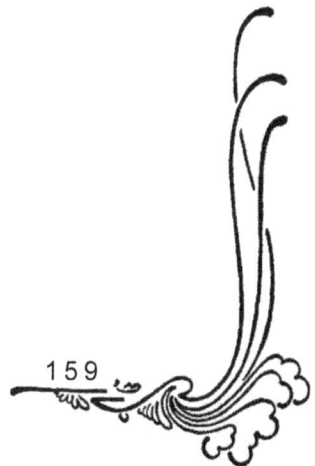

∞

159

"There is nothing
like a dream
to create the future."

~ Victor Hugo

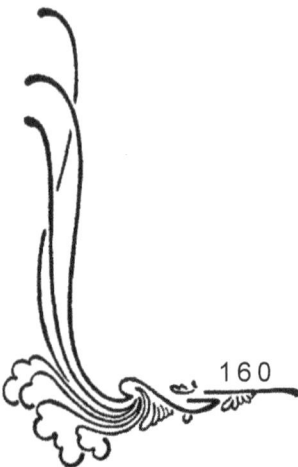

"There is nothing noble
in being superior
to another man.
True nobility
is in being superior
to your previous self."

~ Hindu Proverb via M. Erosa

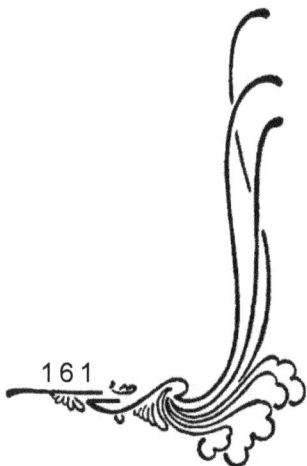

∞

"There are some things
that can be known
but not understood,
but everything
that can be understood
can be known."

~ Brent N. Hunter

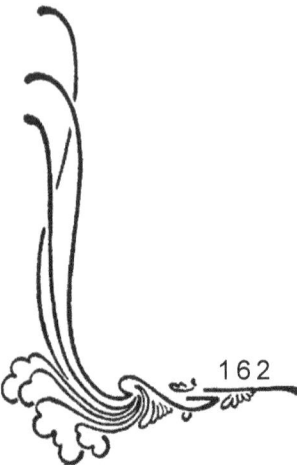

∞

"There was a man
and they called him mad;
the more he gave,
the more he had."

~ John Bunyan

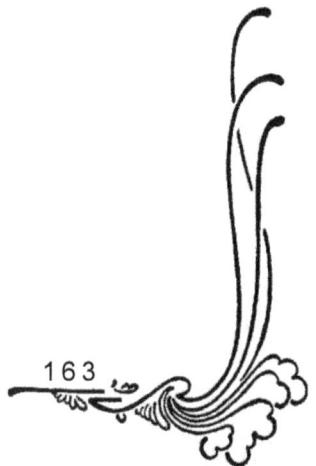

"There was
so much handwriting
on the wall that even the wall
fell down."

~ Christopher Morley

"Think about
what makes you happy.
That's it."

~ Alan Cohen

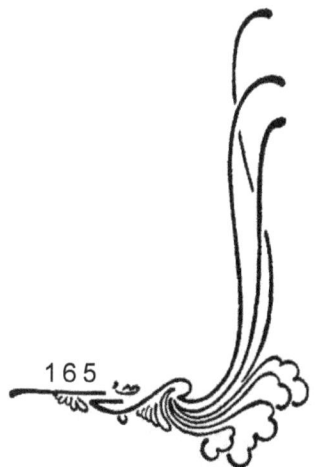

"Try to be like the turtle –
at ease in your own shell."

~ Bill Copeland

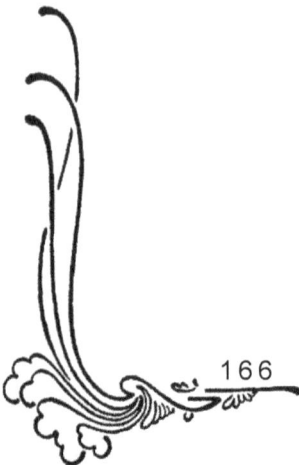

∞

"Think of yourself
as on the threshold
of unparalleled success.
A whole clear, glorious life
lies before you.
Achieve!"

~ Andrew Carnegie

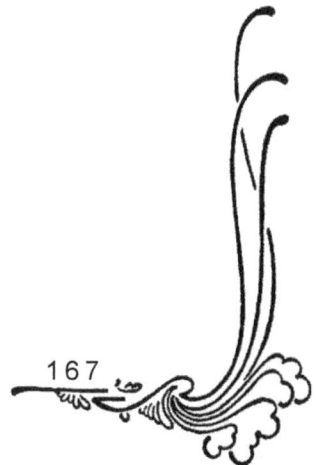

∞

*"Thinking
is the hardest work there is,
which is probably the reason
so few engage in it."*

~ Henry Ford

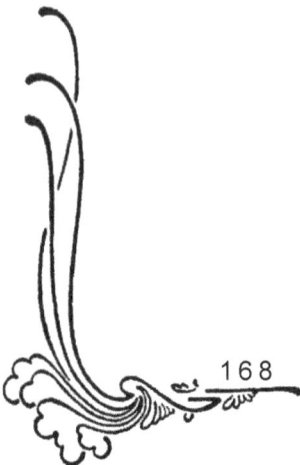

"Those who bring sunshine
into the lives of others,
cannot keep it
from themselves."

~ James Barrie

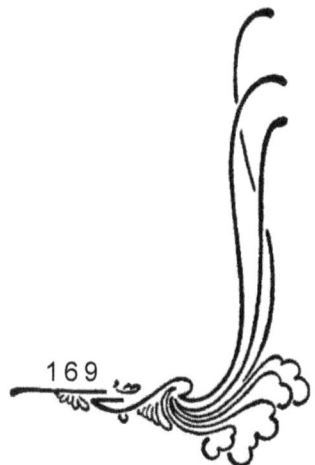

"*Those who dream by day are cognizant of many things which escape those who dream only by night.*"

~ Edgar Allan Poe

∞

"Those who know,
do not speak.
Those who speak,
do not know."

~ Tao Te Ching

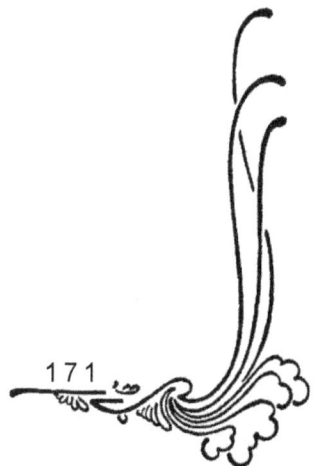

"Those who never retract
their opinions love themselves
more than they love
the truth."

~ Joseph Joubert

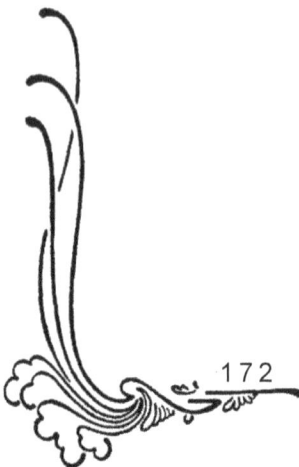

"Those
who stand for nothing
fall for anything."

~ Alexander Hamilton

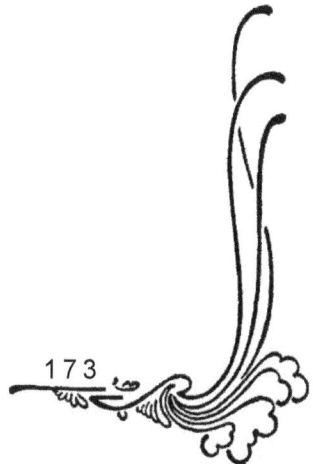

∞

"What lies behind us
and what lies before us are
tiny matters compared to
what lies within us."

~ Ralph Waldo Emerson

"*Thought
is action in rehearsal.*"

~ Sigmund Freud

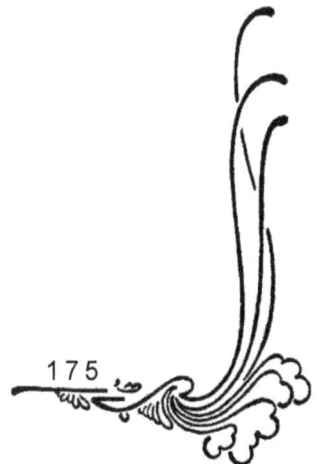

"Thoughts have power.
You can make your world
or break it
by your own thinking."

~ Susan Taylor

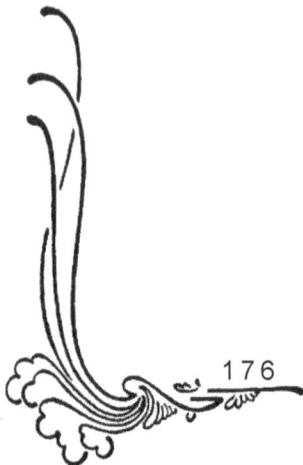

"Thousands of years ago,
cats were worshipped as Gods.
Cats
have never forgotten this."

~ Anonymous

"Three steps in the revelation
of any truth:
(1) it is ridiculed;
(2) it is resisted;
(3) it is considered
self-evident."

~ Arthur Schopenhauer

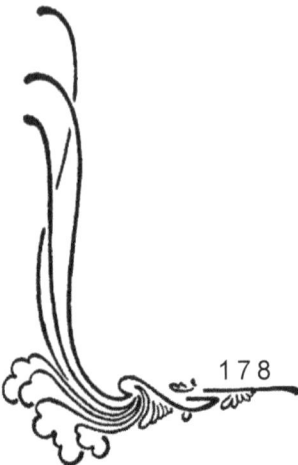

"Three things
can't be long hidden:
The sun, the moon
and the truth."

~ Buddha

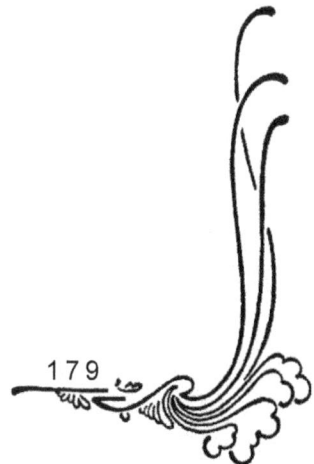

179

"Through the power of love
barriers can be broken...
the other side of the bridge
is definitely worth
the journey."

~ Dea Shandera

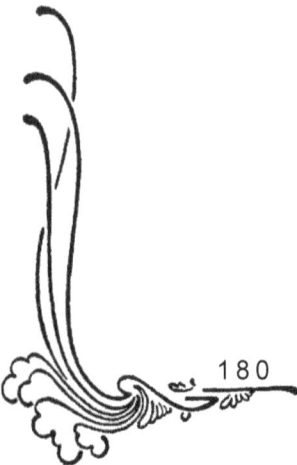

"*Throw your heart
over the fence and the rest
will follow.*"

~ Norman Vincent Peale

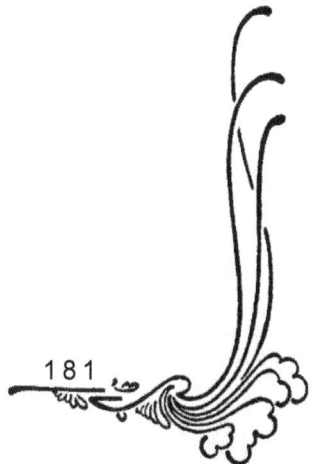

∞

"Time has a wonderful way
of showing us
what really matters."

~ Margaret Peters

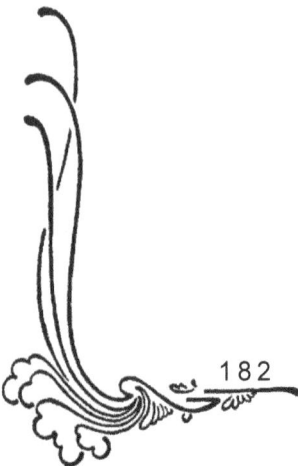

"To a mind that is still,
the whole universe surrenders."

~ Chang Tsu

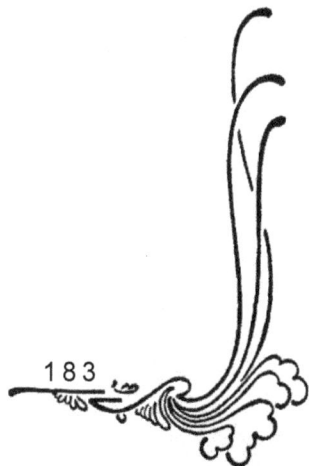

183

"To accomplish great things,
we must dream,
as well as act."

~ Anatole France

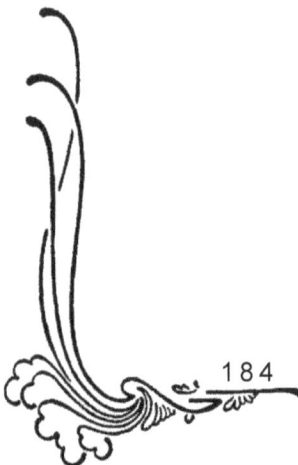

∞

"To achieve the impossible,
it is precisely the unthinkable
that must be thought."

~ Anthony Robbins

185

"To fight fear, act.
To increase fear —
wait, put off, postpone."

~ David J. Schwartz

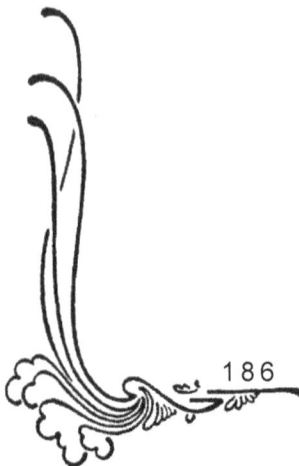

∞

"To keep a lamp burning,
we have to
keep putting oil in it."

~ Mother Teresa

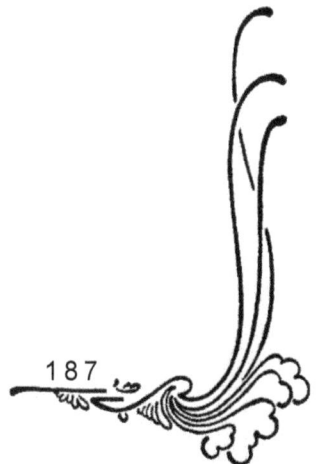

"To know when to go away
and when to come closer
is the key
to any lasting relationship."

~ Doménico Cieri Estrada

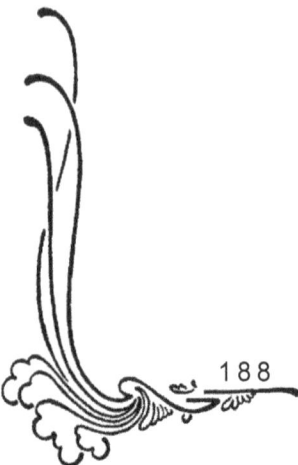

∞

"To love
is to receive a glimpse
of heaven."

~ Karen Sunde

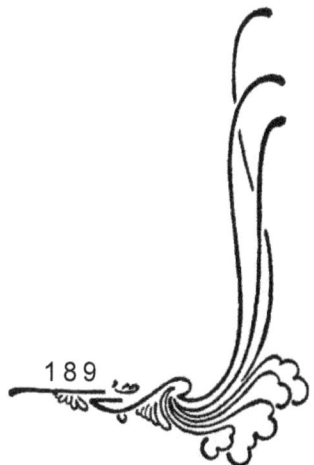

"To love someone deeply
gives you strength.
Being loved
by someone deeply
gives you courage."

~ Lao Tzu

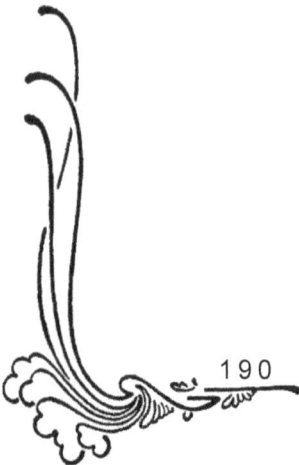

"To me
every hour of the light
and dark is a miracle.
Every cubic inch of space
is a miracle."

~ Walt Whitman

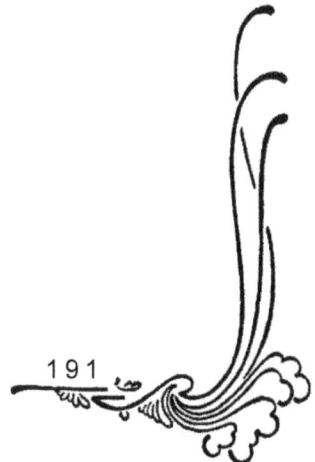

"To perceive
a successful outcome
is to achieve
a successful outcome."

~ Eleesha

"To the world
you may be one person,
but to that one person,
you may be the world."

~ Bill Wilson

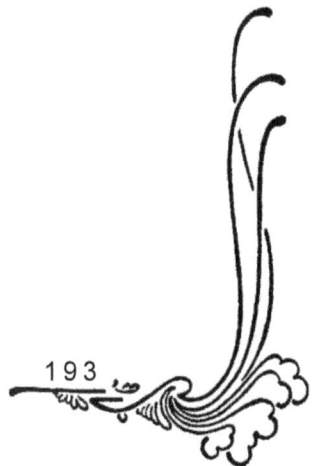

"Today,
give a stranger
one of your smiles.
It may be the only sunshine
he sees all day."

~ H. Jackson Brown, Jr.

∞

"Today is the tomorrow
you worried about yesterday."

~ Ancient Proverb

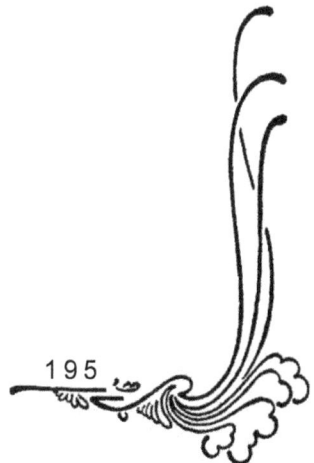

∞

"Today, smile at someone who seems angry or sad and you will have made the world a better place."

~ Brent N. Hunter

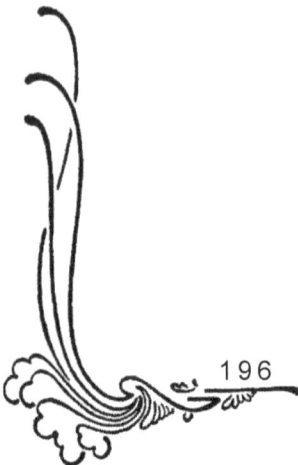

∞

"Tomorrow is often
the busiest day of the week."

~ Spanish Proverb

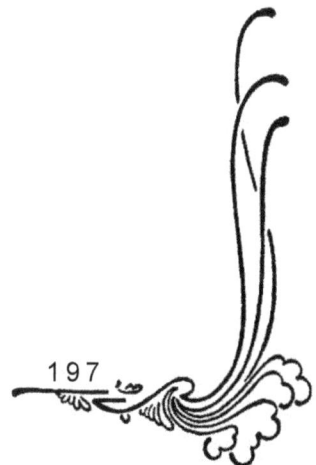

∞

"Trust that little voice
in your head that says,
'Wouldn't it be interesting
if...';
and then do it."

~ Duane Michals

∞

"Trust that still, small voice that says, 'This might work and I'll try it.'"

~ Diane Mariechild

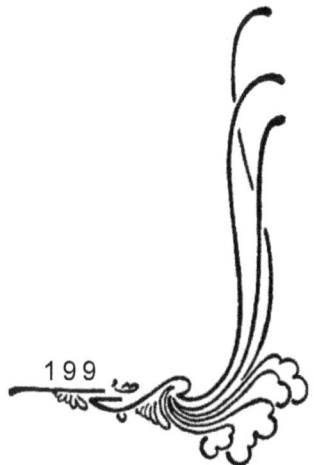

"Trust the dreams
for hidden in them
is the gate to eternity."

~ Kahlil Gibran

∞

"*Always do right.*
This will gratify
some people,
and astonish the rest."

~ Mark Twain

"Trust yourself.
You know more
than you think you do."

~ Benjamin Spock

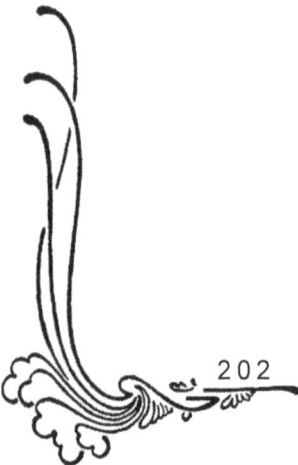

∞

"Trusting our intuition
often saves us from disaster."

~ Anne Wilson Schaef

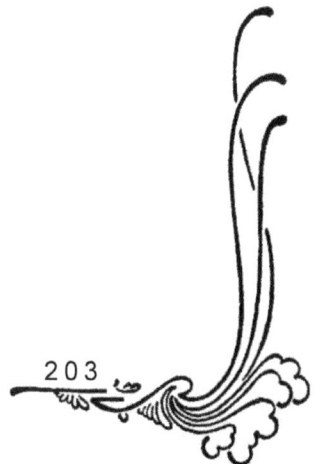

∞

"Truth
is a pathless land."

~ Krishnamurti

∞

"Truth is by nature
self-evident.
As soon as you remove
the cobwebs of ignorance
that surround it,
it shines clear."

~ Mahatma Gandhi

∞

"Try not to become
a person of success,
but a person of value."

~ Albert Einstein

∞

"*Trying times
are no time to quit trying.*"

~ Unknown

"*Turn your wounds into wisdom.*"

~ Oprah Winfrey

∞

"You see things
and say 'Why?'
But I dream things
that never were
and I say 'Why not?'"

~ George Bernard Shaw

∞

"Until you make peace
with who you are,
you'll never be content
with what you have."

~ Doris Mortman

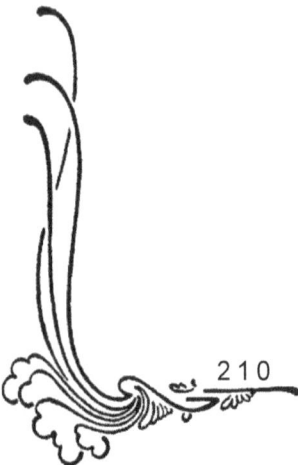

"*Your present circumstances don't determine where you can go; they merely determine where you start.*"

~ Nido Qubein

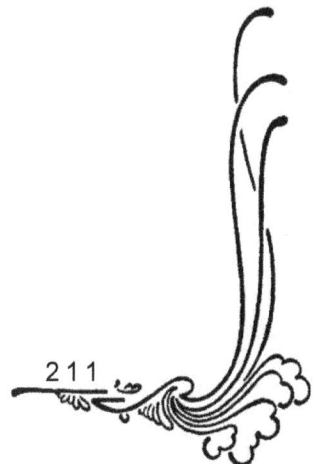

"Vision is the art
of seeing what is invisible
to others."

~ Jonathan Swift

∞

"We all have
our time machines.
Some take us back,
they're called memories.
Some take us forward,
they're called dreams."

~ Jeremy Irons

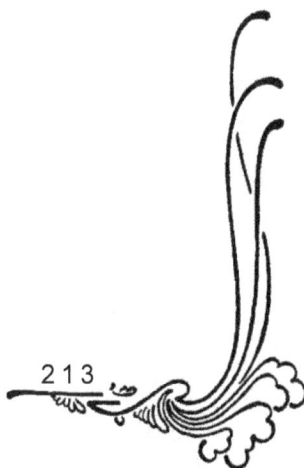

"We are called to be
architects of the future,
not its victims."

~ Buckminster Fuller

"We are here to add
what we can to life,
not to get what we can
from life."

~ William Osler

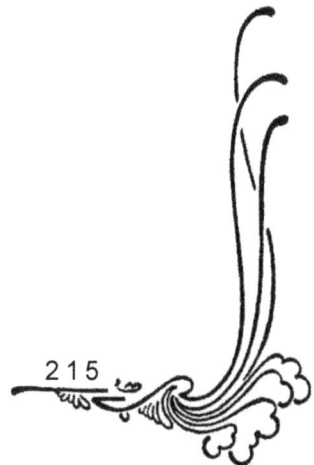

"We are the people
the world has been waiting for
and now is the time
to act as one."

~ Adapted From A Message From The Hopi Elders

∞

"We call them
dumb animals
and so they are,
for they cannot tell you
how they feel,
but they don't suffer less
because they have no words."

~ Anna Sewell

"We can judge
the heart of man
by his treatment of animals."

~ Immanuel Kant

"*He who knows nothing
is closer to the truth
than he whose mind
is filled with falsehoods
and errors.*"

~ Thomas Jefferson

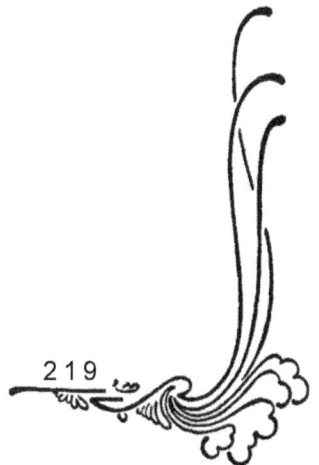

∞

"We cannot
defend freedom abroad
by deserting it at home."

~ Edward R. Murrow

"We cannot hold a torch
to light another's path
without brightening our own."

~ Ben Sweetland

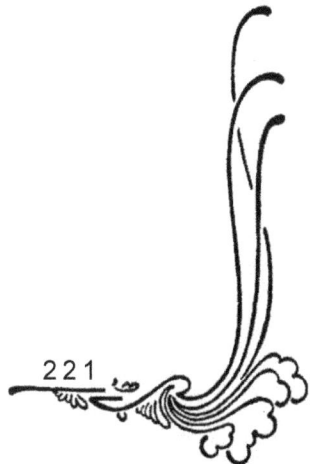

∞

"We choose to go to the moon in this decade and do the other things, not because they are easy, but because they are hard, because that goal will serve to organize and measure the best of our energies and skills..."

~ John F. Kennedy

∞

"We come to love
not by finding
a perfect person,
but by learning to see
an imperfect person perfectly."

~ Sam Keen

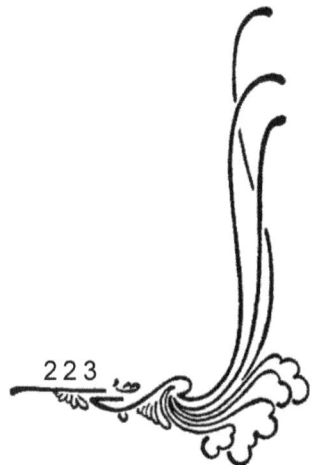

"We live in the 21st century
when literally anything
is possible.
It's irresponsible
to be pessimistic in a field
of infinite possibilities."

~ Brent N. Hunter

∞

"We make a living
by what we get,
we make a life
by what we give."

~ Sir Winston Churchill

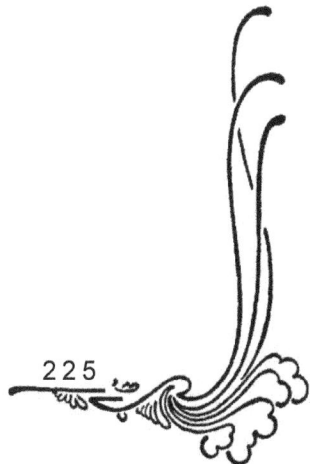

∞

"We make our world
significant
by the courage
of our questions
and by the depth
of our answers."

~ Carl Sagan

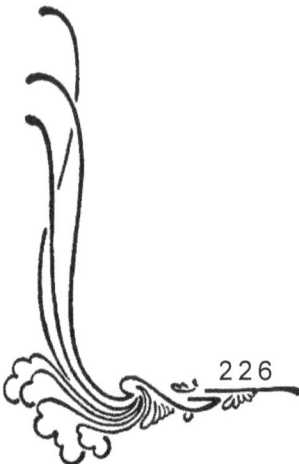

"We must learn
to live together as brothers,
or we will die together
as fools."

~ Martin Luther King, Jr.

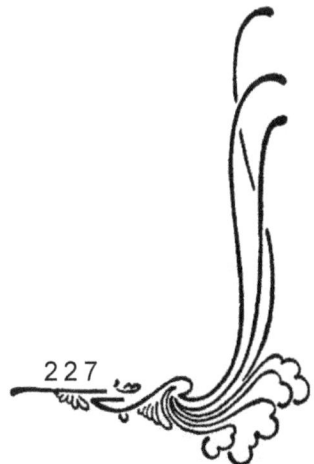

∞

"We must not allow ourselves to become like the system we oppose."

~ Archbishop Desmond Tutu

∞

"We must use time
as a tool,
not as a crutch."

~ John F. Kennedy

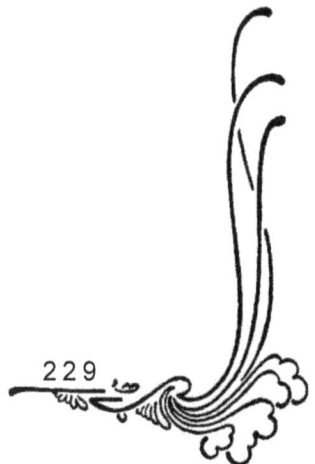

∞

"We seek peace,
knowing that peace
is the climate of freedom."

~ Dwight D. Eisenhower

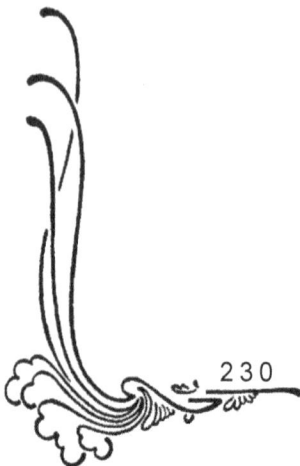

"We think too much
and feel too little."

~ Charlie Chaplin

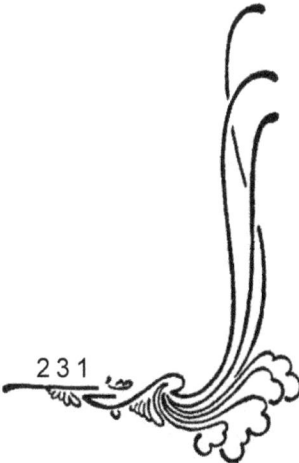

∞

"We want
to change our lives,
but refuse to change
our thoughts,
therefore, we remain bound."

~ James Allen

"We will be known forever
by the tracks we leave."

~ Native-American proverb

∞

233

"Understand that the right
to choose your own path
is a sacred privilege.
Use it.
Dwell in possibility."

~ Oprah Winfrey

∞

"We would accomplish
many more things
if we did not think of them
as impossible."

~ Vince Lombardi

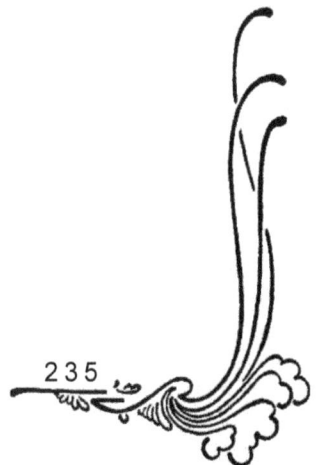

∞

"We would worry less
about what others think of us
if we realized how seldom
they do."

~ Ethel Barrett

"What happens
is not as important as
how you react
to what happens."

~ Thaddeus Golas

∞

237

"What is a weed?
A plant whose virtues
have not yet been discovered."

~ Ralph Waldo Emerson

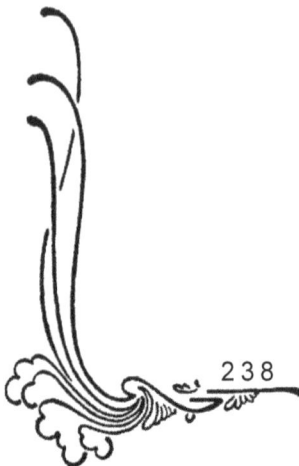

∞

"What sunshine is to flowers, smiles are to humanity."

~ Joseph Addison

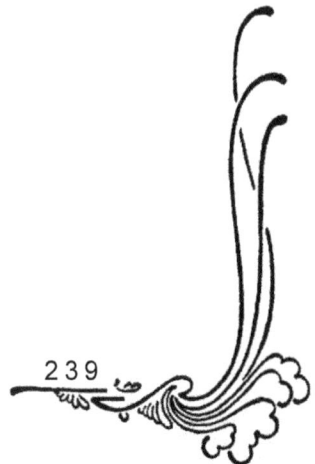

∞

239

"What the caterpillar calls
the end of the world,
the master calls
a butterfly."

~ Richard Bach

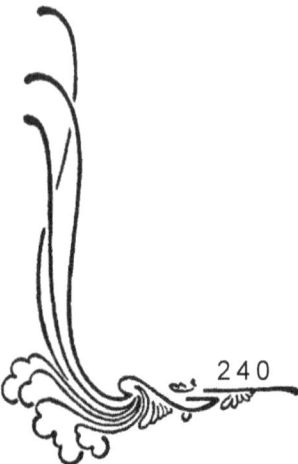

"What this power is,
I cannot say.
All I know
is that it exists."

~ Alexander Graham Bell

∞

"What unites all beings is their desire for happiness."

~ HH The Dalai Lama

"What we leave behind
is not engraved
in stone monuments,
but woven into the lives
of others."

~ Pericles

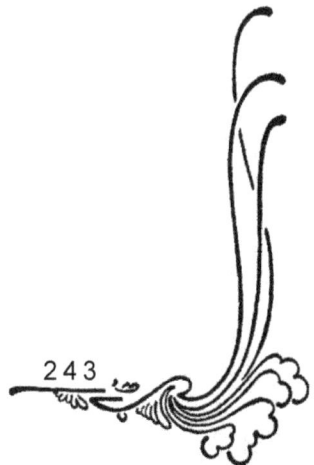

"What you see
depends on what
you're looking for."

~ Unknown

"Whatever the mind
can conceive and believe,
it can achieve."

~ Napoleon Hill

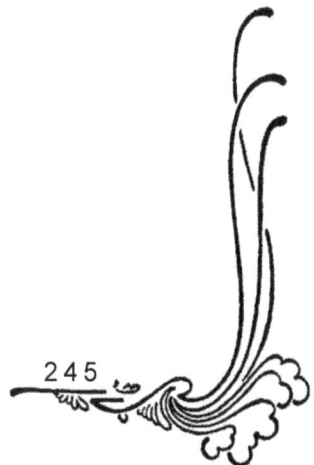

∞

"Whatever you can do,
or dream you can, begin it.
Boldness has genius, power,
and magic in it."

~Johann Wolfgang von Goethe

∞

"Clouds come floating into my life, no longer to carry rain or to usher storm, but to add color to my sunset sky."

~ Rabindranath Tagore

"What's popular
isn't always right
and what's right
isn't always popular!"

~ Anonymous

"What's the difference
between a cat and a dog?
Dogs have masters
and cats have staff."

~ Unknown

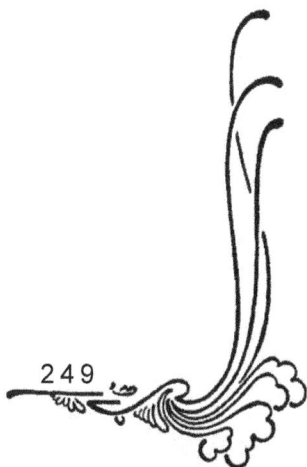

"When it gets dark enough,
you can see the stars."

~ Lee Salk

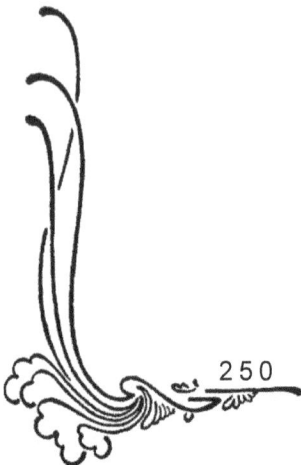

"When mind, body, and spirit are in harmony, happiness is the natural result."

~ Deepak Chopra

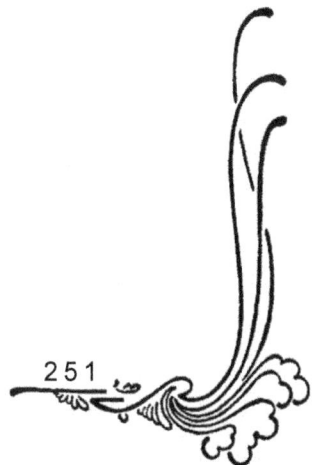

"When people go to work,
they shouldn't have to leave
their hearts at home."

~ Betty Bender

"When the mind
is nowhere it is everywhere.
When it occupies one tenth,
it is absent
in the other nine tenths."

~ Takuan Sōhō

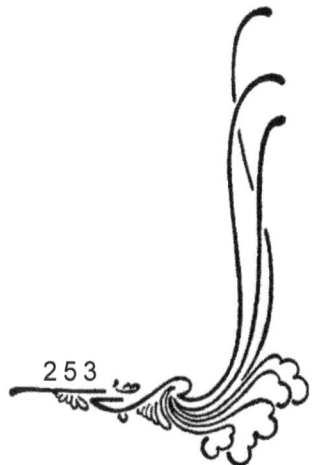

"When the power of love overcomes the love of power, the world will know peace."

~ Jimi Hendrix

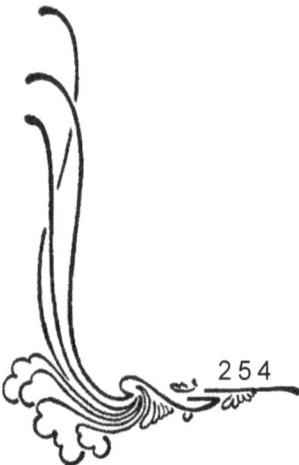

"When the pupil is ready,
the teacher will appear."

~ Unknown

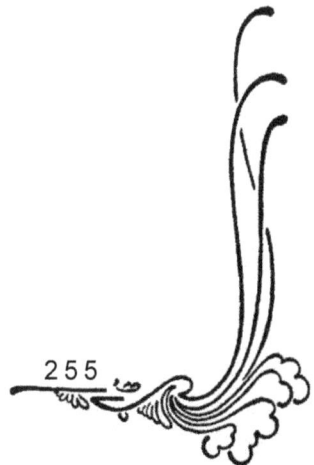

"When the sense of 'me' disappears completely, duality vanishes in ecstasy."

~ Ramesh Balsekar

"When you give yourself permission to be open, real and brilliant around others, you give others permission to be open, real and brilliant around you."

~ Robin Sharma

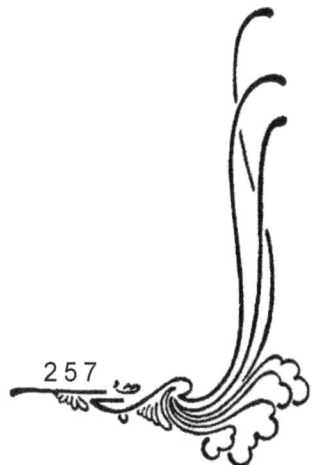

"When walking through
the 'valley of shadows',
remember, a shadow is cast
by a light."

~ H.K. Barclay

"When we can't find peace
in ourselves,
it is vain
to look for it elsewhere."

~ Proverb

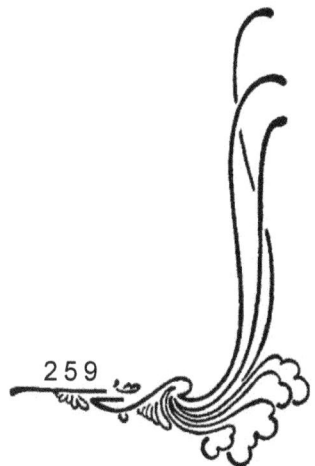

"When we dream alone,
it's a dream,
when we dream together,
it's reality."

~ Unknown

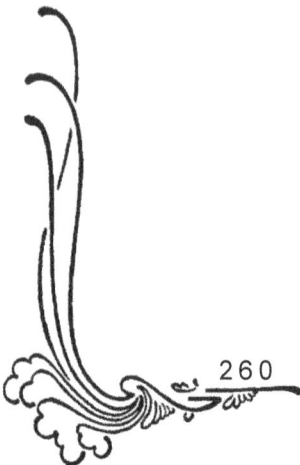

"When we tug
at a single thing in nature,
we find it attached
to the rest of the world."

~ John Muir

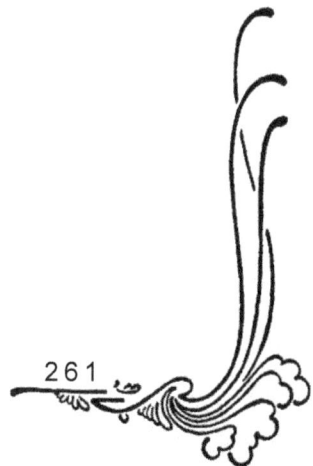

"When you have only two
pennies left in the world,
buy a loaf of bread
with one, and a lily
with the other."

~ Unknown

"When you know something,
say what you know.
When you don't
know something,
say that you don't know."

~ Confucius

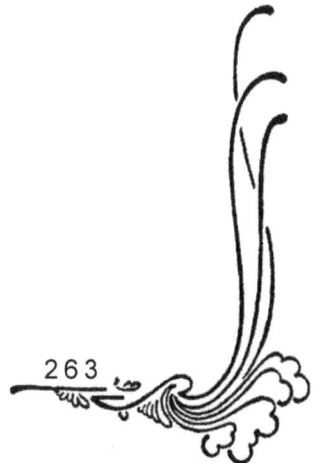

263

"When you make peace
with yourself,
you make peace
with the world."

~ Maha Ghosananda

"When you teach your son,
you teach your son's son."

~ The Talmud

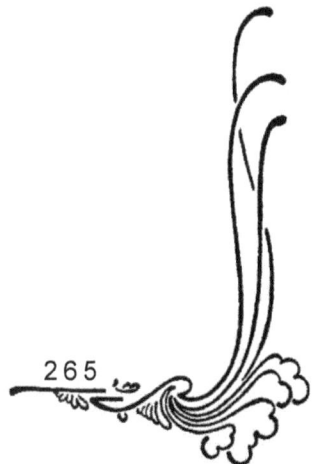

"Someone is sitting in the shade today because someone planted a tree a long time ago."

~ Warren Buffett

∞

"Wherever you go,
no matter what the weather,
always bring
your own sunshine."

~ Anthony J. D'Angelo

∞

"Whether you think you can or cannot, you're right."

~ Henry Ford

"Who looks outside,
dreams;
who looks inside,
awakens."

~ C.G. Jung

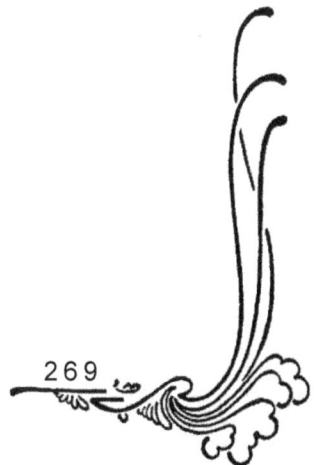

"Who we are never changes.
Who we think we are does."

~ Mary S. Almanac

∞

"*I am prepared for the worst but hope for the best.*"

~ Benjamin Disraeli

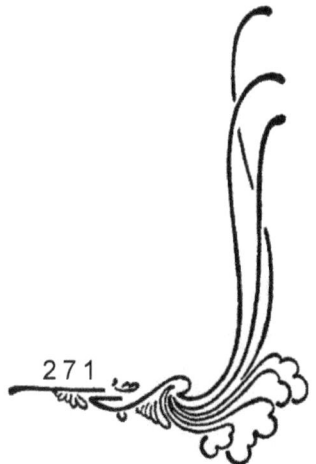

∞

271

"Everyone must row
with the oars he has."

~ English proverb

"Why not go out on a limb, that's where all the fruit is!"

~ Mark Twain

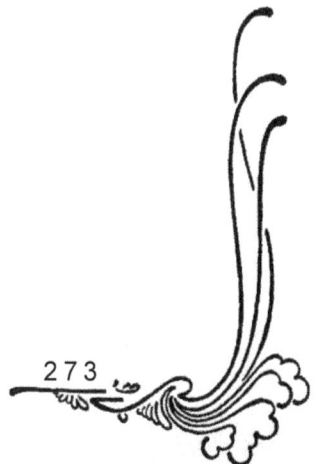

"*Follow your bliss and the universe will open doors where there were only walls.*"

~ Joseph Campbell

"Without deviation
from the norm,
progress is not possible."

~ Frank Zappa

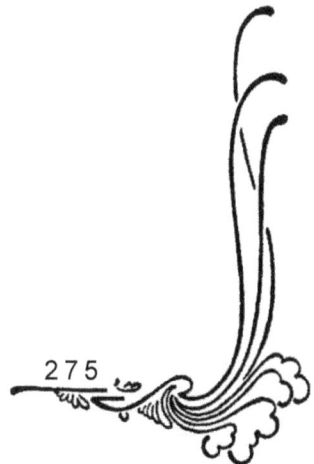

"Wondering how
a water bottle with the tagline
"trickled through mountains
for centuries"
can have an expiration date
of next year."

~ L. Ricardo

"Words have wings...
so speak good things!"

~ Anonymous

"Work is love made visible."

~ Kahlil Gibran

∞

"Yesterday is history.
Tomorrow is a mystery.
Today is a gift.
That is why we call it
The Present."

~ Unknown

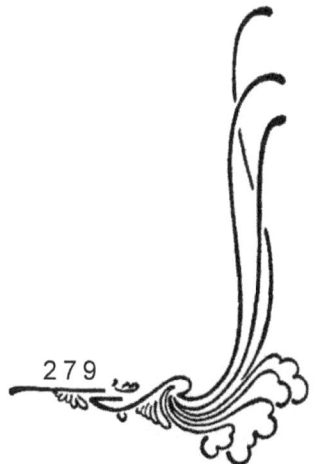

"You already have
the precious mixture
that will make you well.
Use it."

~ Jalāl ad-Dīn Muhammad Balkhī "Rumi"

∞

*"You are here
to enable the divine purpose
of the universe to unfold.
That is how important
you are!"*

~ Eckhart Tolle

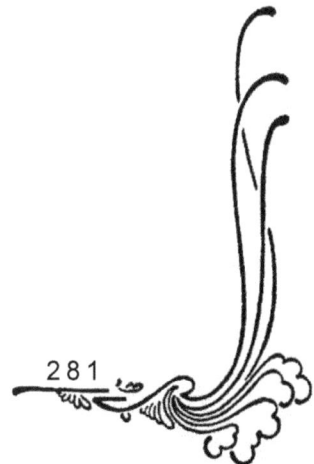

∞

"You can never plan the future by the past."

~ Edmund Burke

"You cannot be lonely
if you like the person
you are alone with."

~ Wayne Dyer

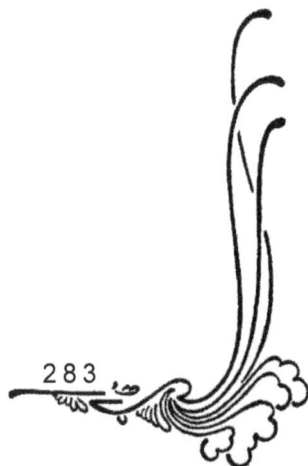

"You cannot do
a kindness too soon,
for you never know how soon
it will be too late."

~ Ralph Waldo Emerson

*"You cannot escape
the responsibility of tomorrow
by evading it today."*

~ Abraham Lincoln

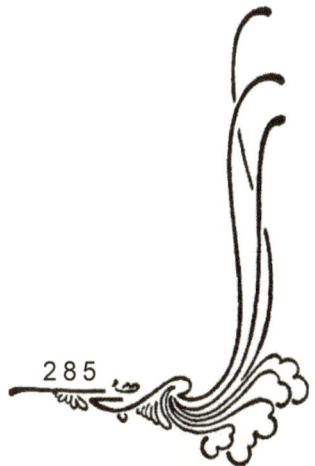

∞

"You can't hit a target
you cannot see,
and you cannot see a target
you do not have."

~ Zig Ziglar

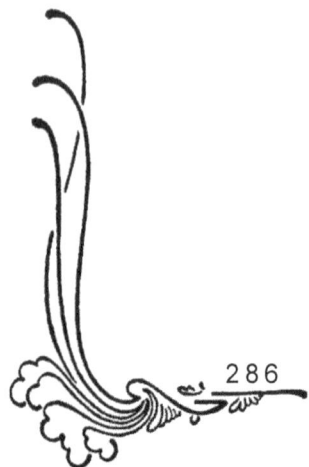

"*You can't lose weight
by talking about it.
You have to keep
your mouth shut.*"

~ Unknown

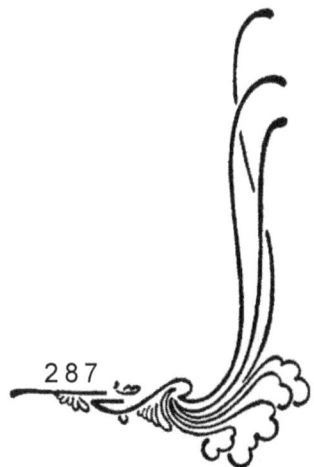

"*You can't separate peace
from freedom
because no one can be
at peace unless he has
his freedom.*"

~ Malcolm X

"You don't have a soul.
You are a soul.
You have a body."

~ C.S. Lewis

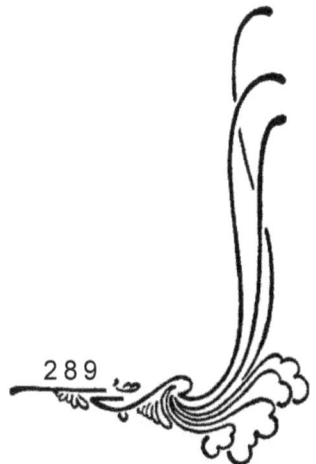

"We need people
who can dream of things
that never were."

~ John F. Kennedy

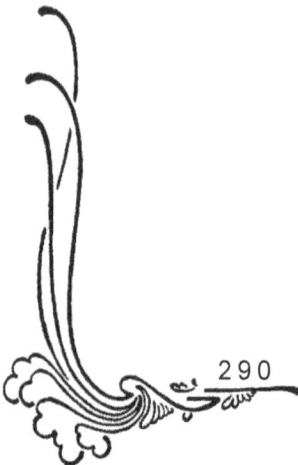

∞

"You don't have to be anti-man to be pro-woman."

~ Jane Galvin Lewis

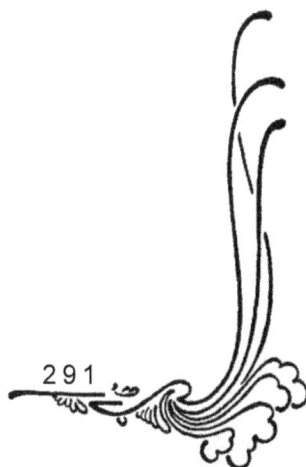

∞

"You don't have to see
the whole staircase,
just take the first step."

~ Martin Luther King, Jr.

∞

"You don't need
endless time
and perfect conditions.
Do it now.
Do it for twenty minutes
and watch your heart
start beating."

~ Barbara Sher

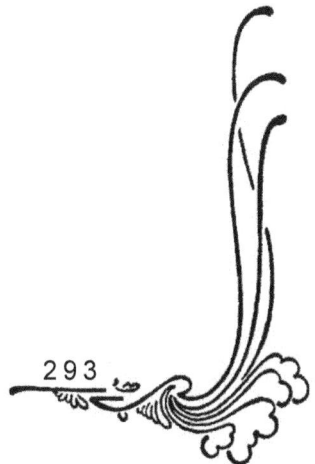

"You don't stop laughing
because you grow older.
You grow older
because you stop laughing."

~ Maurice Chevalier

∞

"You have no control over what the other guy does. You only have control over what you do."

~ A.J. Kitt

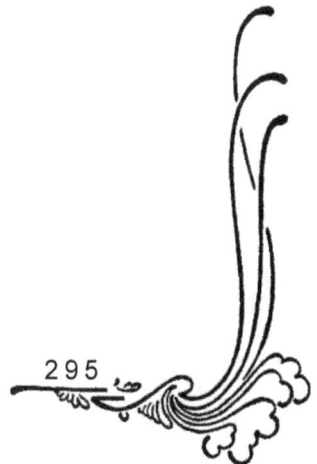

"You have to
let it all go, Neo.
Fear, doubt, and disbelief.
Free your mind."

~ Morpheus, from "The Matrix"

∞

"*You have to take it
as it happens,
but you should try
to make it happen
the way you want to take it.*"

~ Unknown

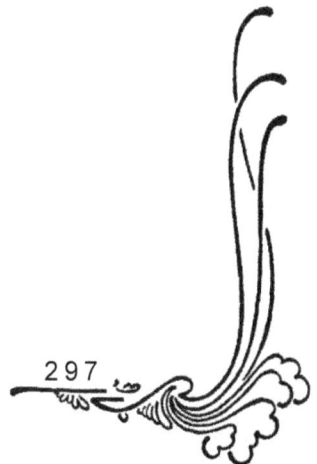

"You may say
I'm a dreamer,
I'm not the only one.
I hope someday you join us,
and the world will
live as one."

~ John Lennon

"*You never fail until you stop trying.*"

~ Albert Einstein

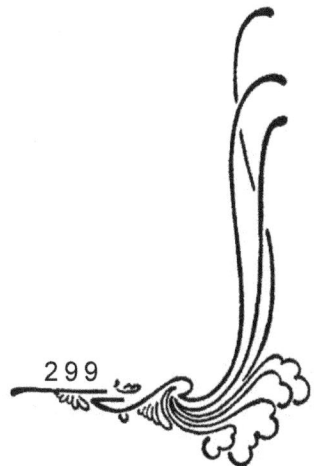

∞

299

*"You were born with wings.
Why prefer to crawl
through life?"*

~ Jalāl ad-Dīn Muhammad Balkhī "Rumi"

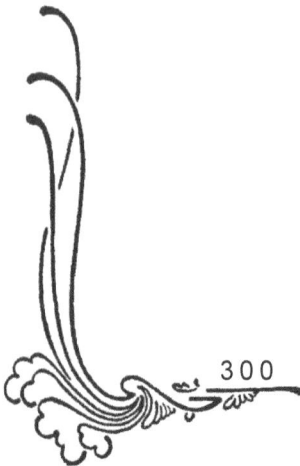

∞

"You will fear the darkness
only to the extent
that you yourself are not
providing light."

~ Marianne Williamson

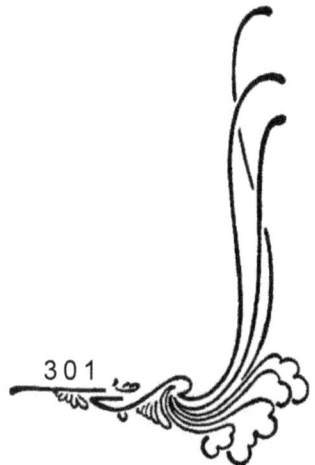

301

*"You'll see it
when you believe it."*

~ Wayne Dyer

"Your imagination
is your preview
of life's coming attractions."

~ Albert Einstein

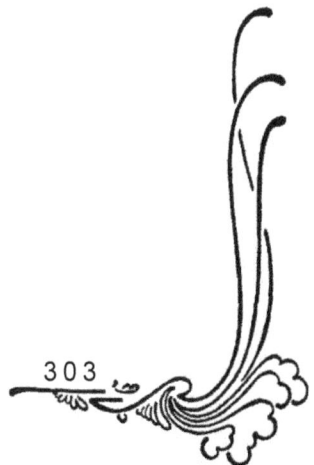

∞

303

*"Your most
unhappy customers
are your greatest source
of learning."*

~ Bill Gates

"Look within. Within is the fountain of good, and it will ever bubble up, if thou wilt ever dig."

~ Marcus Aurelius

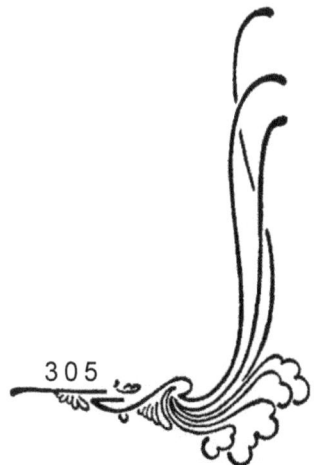

"Your purpose
is what you say it is."

~ Neale Donald Walsch

∞

*"Your soul
has but one gift to give
and it's called inspiration."*

~ Mike Perras

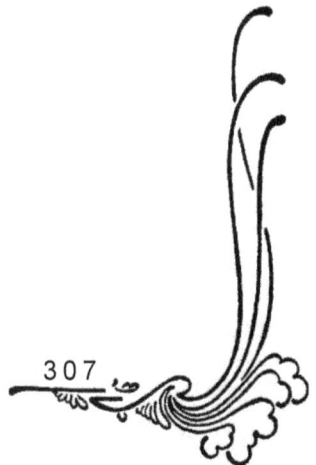

"*Your spiritual practice
is for just one day
to not share what is wrong.
Just for one day,
do not share what is wrong.*"

~ Unknown

"Your thoughts are the architects of your destiny."

~ David O. McKay

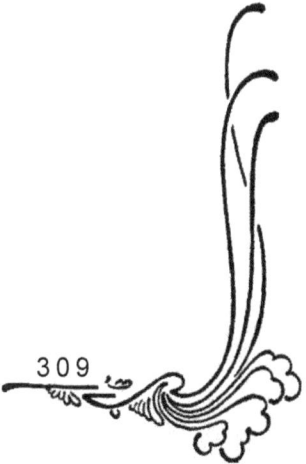

*"Your vision
will become clear
only when you look into
your heart.
Who looks outside, dreams.
Who looks inside, awakens."*

~ C.G. Jung

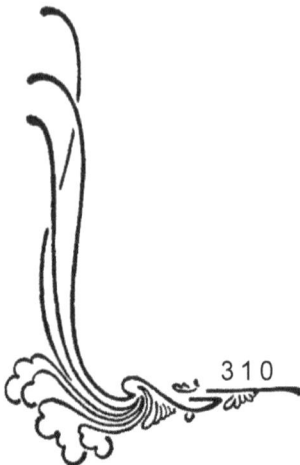

*"I don't believe in failure.
It is not failure
if you enjoyed the process."*

~ Oprah Winfrey

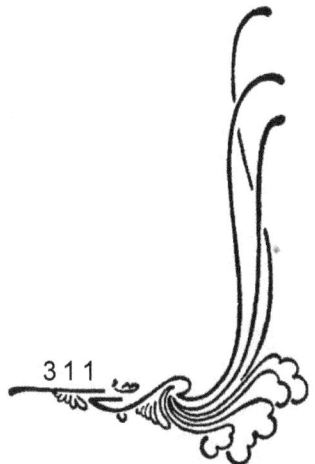

∞

"We can be knowledgeable
with other men's knowledge,
but we cannot be wise
with other men's wisdom."

~ Michel de Montaigne

∞

"*Big things*
have small beginnings."

~ David, from "Prometheus"

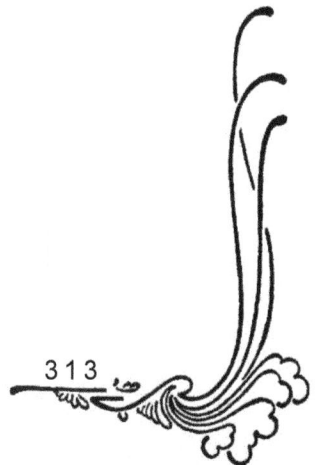

∞

"If your actions
inspire others to dream more,
learn more, do more
and become more,
you are a leader."

~ John Quincy Adams

"*Every production of genius
must be the production
of enthusiasm.*"

~ Benjamin Disraeli

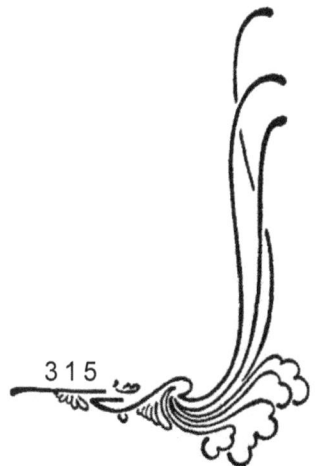

∞

315

"*Leadership is an opportunity to serve. It is not a trumpet call to self-importance.*"

~ J. Donald Walters

"Success consists of
going from failure to failure
without loss of enthusiasm."

~ Sir Winston Churchill

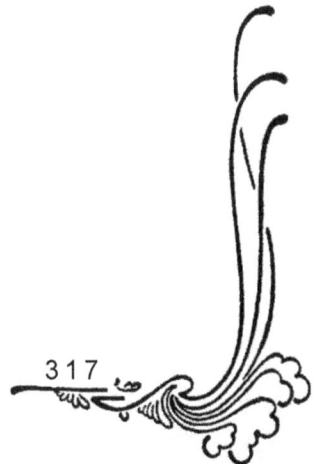

∞

317

"The man
who does things
makes many mistakes,
but he never makes
the biggest mistake of all —
doing nothing."

~ Benjamin Franklin

∞

"Do
what you are afraid to do."

~ Ralph Waldo Emerson

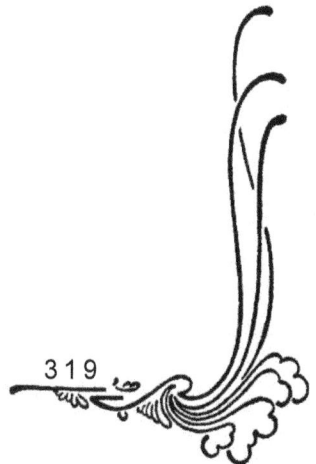

∞

"Deciding what NOT to do
is just as important
as deciding what to do."

~ Archie B. Parrish

"*Let me tell you the secret
that has led me to my goal:
My strength lies solely
in my tenacity.*"

~ Louis Pasteur

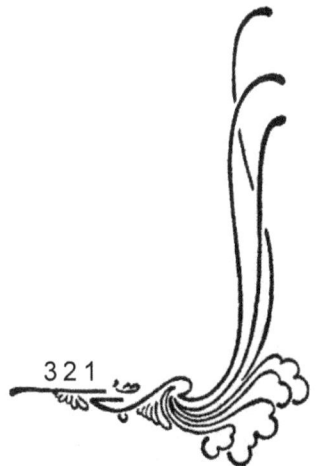

∞

"Nothing is interesting
if you're not interested."

~ Helen MacInness

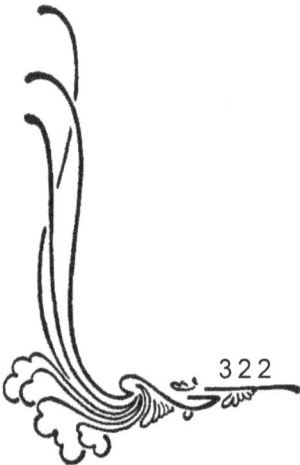

"Things which matter most
must never be at the mercy
of things which matter least."

~ Johann Wolfgang von Goethe

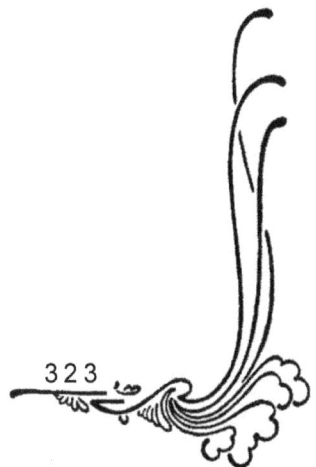

∞

"*Maturity
is the capacity
to endure uncertainty.*"

~ John Finley

324

"The greatest of faults,
I should say,
is to be conscious of none."

~ Thomas Carlyle

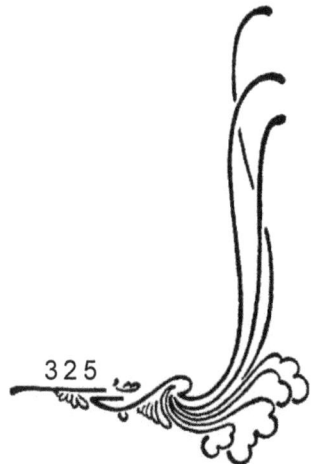

∞

"A happy thought
is like a seed that sows
positivity for all to reap."

~ Miriam Muhammad

∞

"Darkness
cannot drive out darkness;
only light can do that.
Hate cannot drive out hate;
only love can do that."

~ Martin Luther King, Jr.

∞

"A problem can't be resolved
at the same level
of consciousness
that created it."

~ Albert Einstein

∞

"*Success seems to be largely a matter of hanging on after others have let go*."

~ William Feather

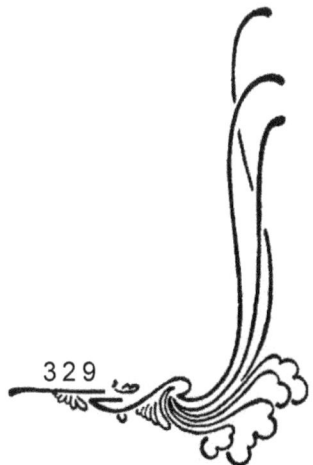

*"The future depends
on what we do in the present."*

~ Mahatma Gandhi

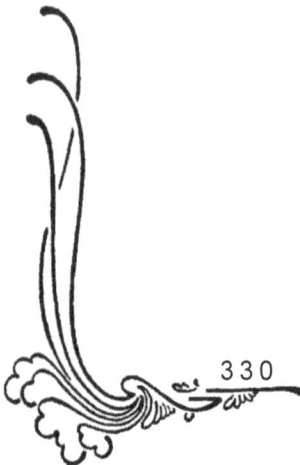

∞

"Your fears are not walls,
but hurdles.
Courage is not
the absence of fear,
but the conquering of it."

~ Dan Millman

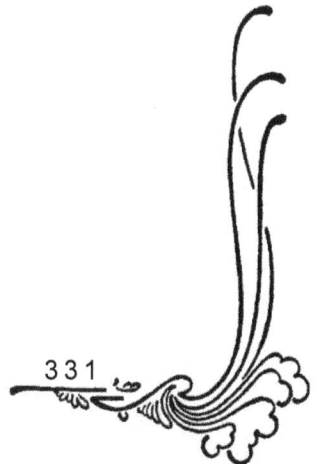

"Courage is doing
what you're afraid to do.
There can be no courage
unless you're scared."

~ Edward Vernon Rickenbacker

"Leadership and learning
are indispensable
to each other."

~ John F. Kennedy

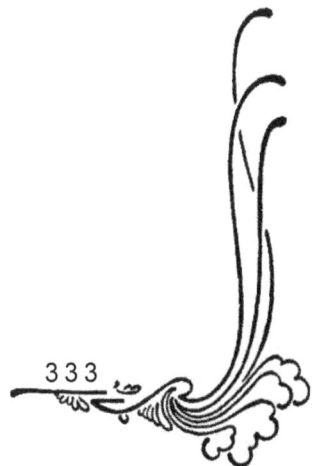

∞

"Your life
is what your thoughts
make it."

~ Marcus Aurelius

∞

"*People are not disturbed
by things, but by the view
they take of them.*"

~ Epictetus

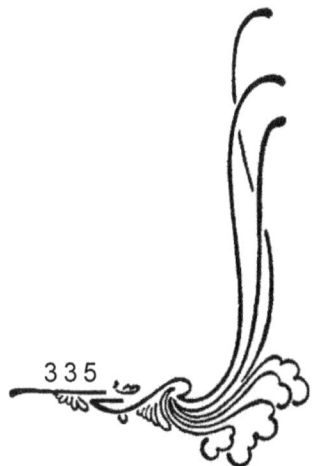

"*People seem not to see
that their opinion
of the world
is also a confession
of character.*"

~ Ralph Waldo Emerson

∞

"Stubbornly persist,
and you will find that the
limits of your stubbornness
go well beyond
the stubbornness
of your limits."

~ Robert Brault

∞

337

"The only difference
between a good day
and a bad day
is your attitude."

~ Dennis S. Brown

∞

"Non-violence
is a sign of strength,
self-confidence and truth."

~ HH The Dalai Lama

"A small body
of determined spirits fired by
an unquenchable faith
in their mission
can alter the course
of history."

~ Mahatma Gandhi

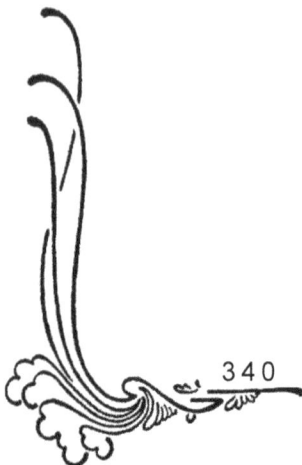

"The soul has been given
its own ears to hear things
that the mind
does not understand."

~ Jalāl ad-Dīn Muhammad Balkhī "Rumi"

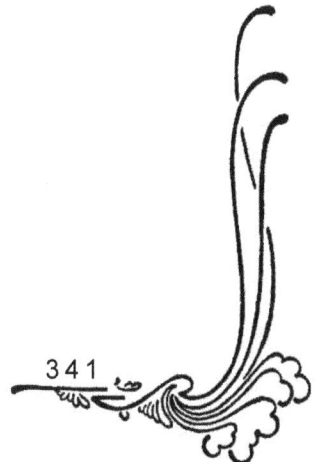

∞

341

"We build too many walls
and not enough bridges."

~ Isaac Newton

"So often times it happens,
that we live our life
in chains...
and we never even know
we have the key."

~ The Eagles, "Already Gone"

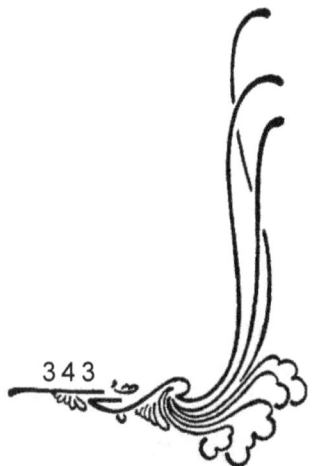

∞

343

"Those who danced
were thought to be insane
by those who could not hear
the music."

~ Friedrich Nietzsche

"Take calculated risks.
That is quite different
from being rash."

~ General George S. Patton

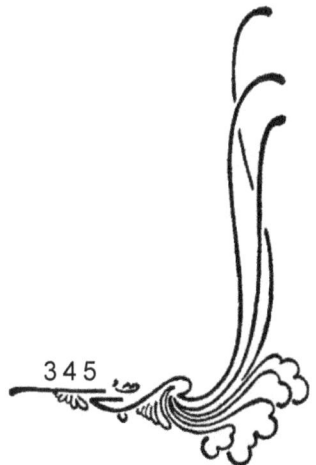

∞

"The talent of success
is nothing more than
doing what you can do,
well."

~ Henry W. Longfellow

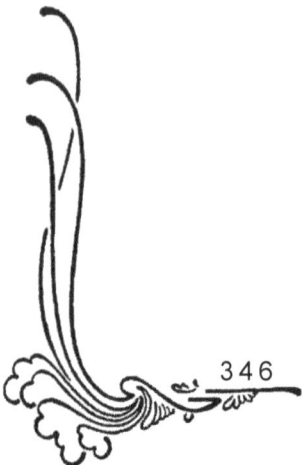

"*A smile
is your greatest social asset.*"

~ Zig Ziglar

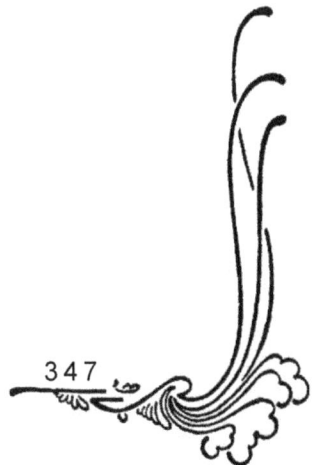

"To climb steep hills
requires a slow pace at first."

~ William Shakespeare

∞

"There is only one success —
to be able to spend your life
in your own way."

~ Christopher Morley

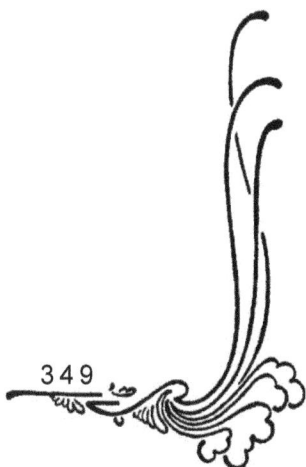

∞

"Today is the first day
of the rest of your life."

~ Charles Dederich

"*All that is gold
does not glitter,
not all those who wander
are lost.*"

~ J.R.R. Tolkien

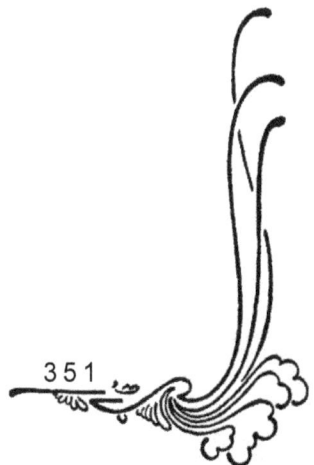

"You must not
lose faith in humanity.
Humanity is an ocean;
if a few drops
of the ocean are dirty,
the ocean does not
become dirty."

~ Mahatma Gandhi

∞

"The secret of genius
is to carry
the spirit of the child
into old age."

~ Aldous Huxley

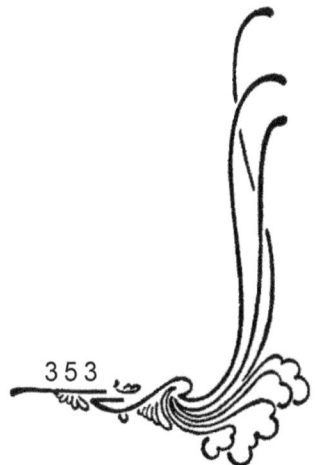

∞

"Look for the answer
inside your question."

~ Jalāl ad-Dīn Muhammad Balkhī "Rumi"

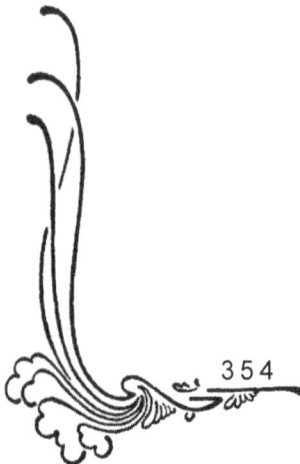

∞

"Dismiss
what insults your soul."

~ Walt Whitman

"*Knowing yourself*
is the beginning
of all wisdom."

~ Aristotle

"The eagle
that is flying high in the sky
should not forget
that it should
come down one day
to see its shadow."

~ Padmasambhava

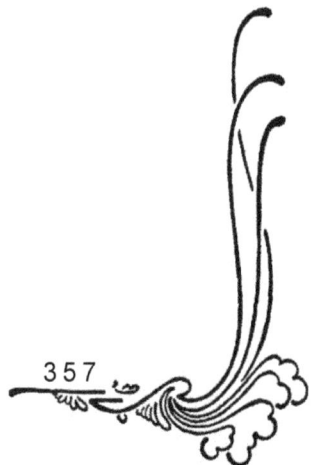

∞

"The truth is like a lion.
You don't have to defend it.
Let it loose.
It will defend itself."

~ St. Augustine

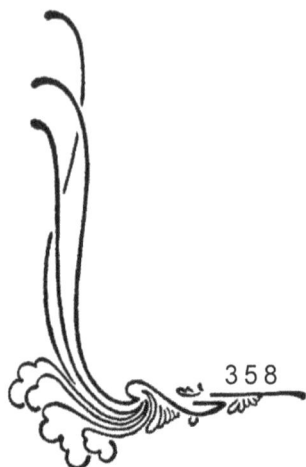

358

*"You yourself
are your own obstacle,
rise above yourself."*

~ Hafiz

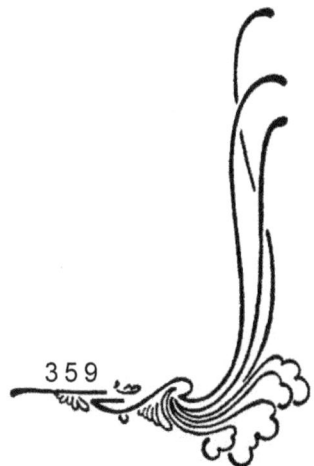

359

"The present moment
is the only moment
available to us,
and it is the door
to all moments."

~ Thich Nhât Hanh

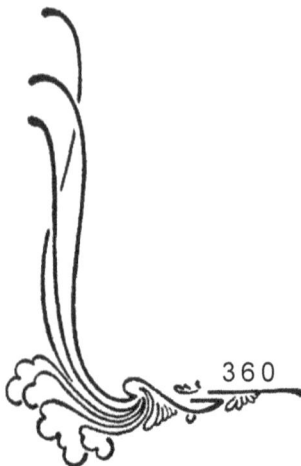

∞

"The best way
to find yourself
is to lose yourself
in the service of others."

~ Mahatma Gandhi

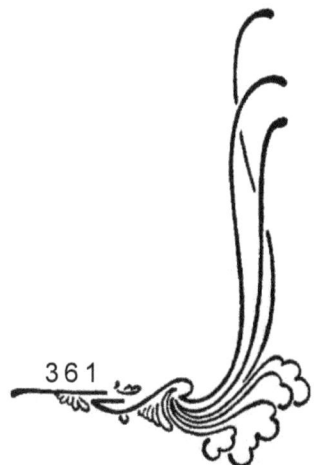

∞

361

"Help one person at a time,
and always start with
the person nearest you."

~ Mother Teresa

∞

"Let me, O let me bathe
my soul in colors;
let me swallow the sunset
and drink the rainbow."

~ Kahlil Gibran

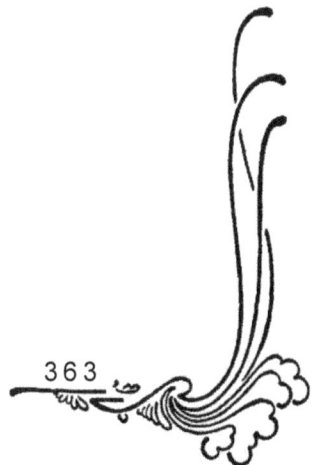

∞

363

"The eye
through which I see God
is the same eye
through which God sees me."

~ Meister Eckhart

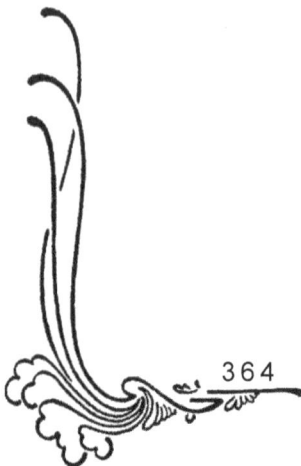

∞

"Remember,
there's no such thing
as a small act of kindness.
Every act creates a ripple
with no logical end."

~ Scott Adams

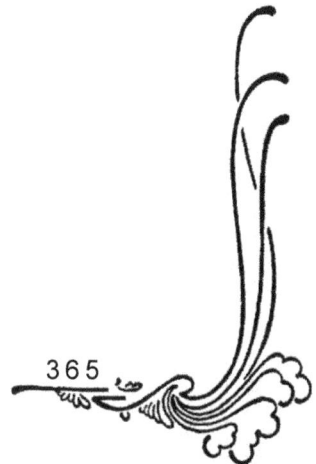

365

"There is a voice
that doesn't use words.
Listen."

~ Jalāl ad-Dīn Muhammad Balkhī "Rumi"

∞

"Never doubt
that a small group
of thoughtful,
committed citizens
can change the world.
Indeed, it is the only thing
that ever has."

~ Margaret Meade

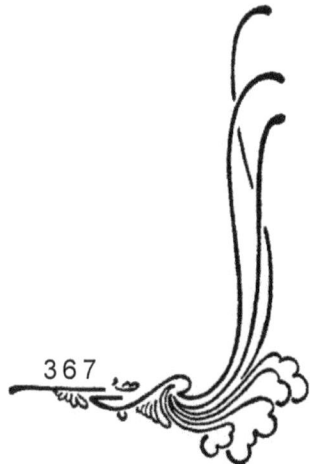

∞

"You miss every shot
that you never take."

~ Michael Jordan

∞

"*Sometimes,*
a cigar is just a cigar."

~ Sigmund Freud

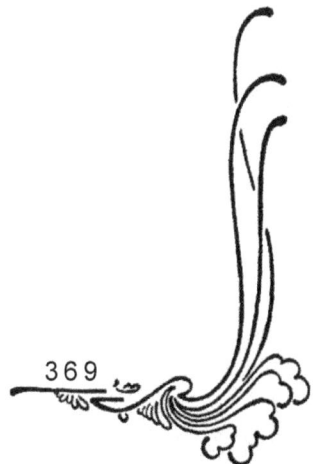

∞

"*Your purpose in life*
is to find your purpose
and give your whole heart
and soul to it."

~ Buddha

370

"Wholeness is not achieved
by cutting off
a portion of one's being,
but by integration
of the contraries."

~ C.G. Jung

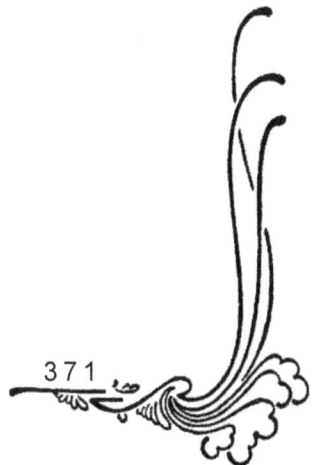

"Whatever you are,
be a good one."

~ Abraham Lincoln

∞

"When you reach the top,
keep climbing."

~ Zen saying

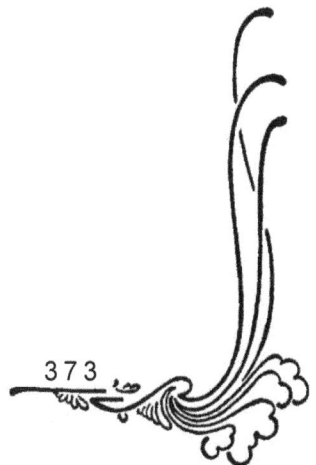

"The young man
knows the rules,
but the old man knows
the exceptions."

~ Oliver Wendell Holmes

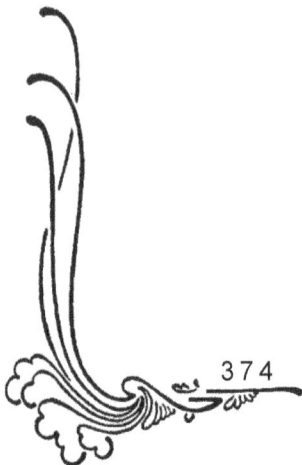

∞

"*Anger is
only one letter short
of danger.*"

~ Anonymous

"The best answer to anger
is silence."

~ Anonymous

"*Those
who abandon their dreams
will discourage yours.*"

~ Anonymous

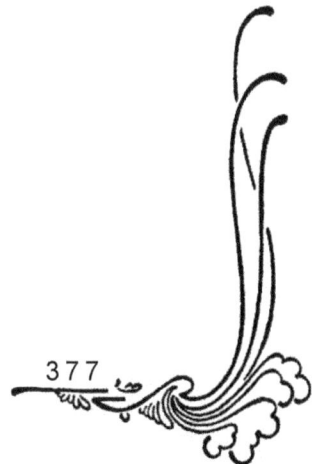

"Instead of complaining
that the rose bush
is full of thorns,
be happy that the thorn bush
has roses."

~ Proverb

"*Be like a duck.*
Calm on the surface,
but paddling like the dickens
underneath."

~ Michael Caine

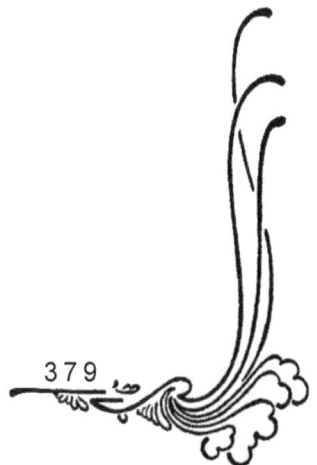

∞

"Nothing endures
but change."

~ Heraclitus

"The most powerful agent
of change
is a change of heart."

~ B. J. Marshall

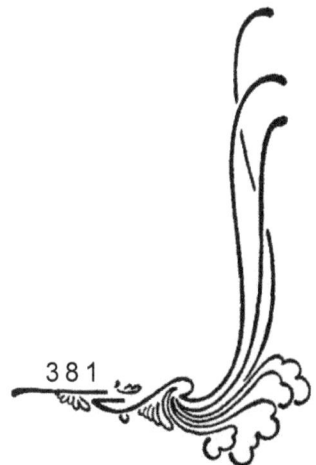

"This is no time
for ease and comfort.
It is time to
dare and endure."

~ Sir Winston Churchill

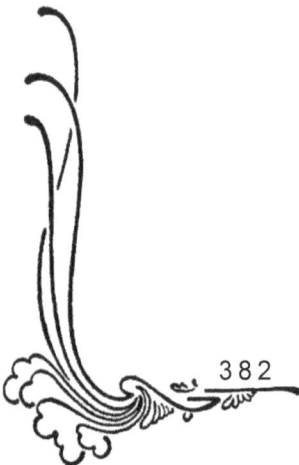

∞

"Dance first, think later. It's the natural order."

~ Samuel Beckett

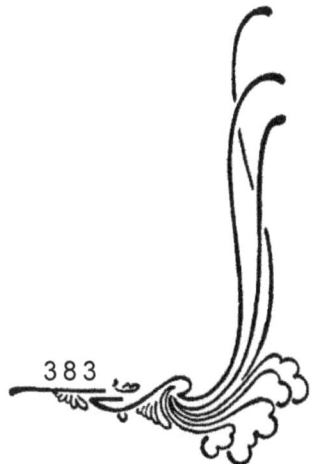

∞

"If you can walk,
you can dance.
If you can talk,
you can sing."

~ Zimbabwean proverb

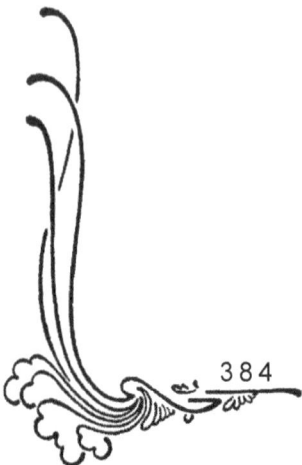

∞

"When you get to
the end of your rope,
tie a knot and hang on."

~ Franklin D. Roosevelt

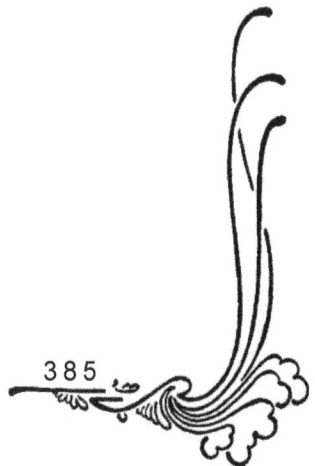

∞

*"Little by little,
one walks far."*

~ Peruvian proverb

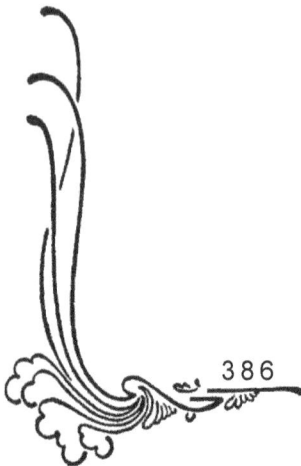

"Those who have
the privilege to know,
have the duty to act."

~ Albert Einstein

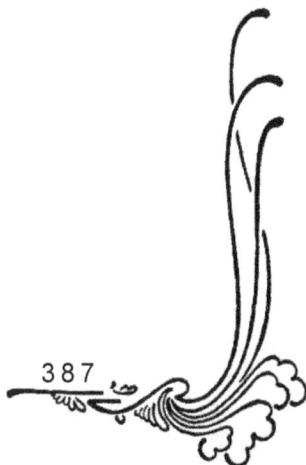

∞

"Every day is a journey,
and the journey itself
is home."

~ Matsuo Bashō

388

"There are no strangers,
only friends
you haven't met yet."

~ HH The Dalai Lama

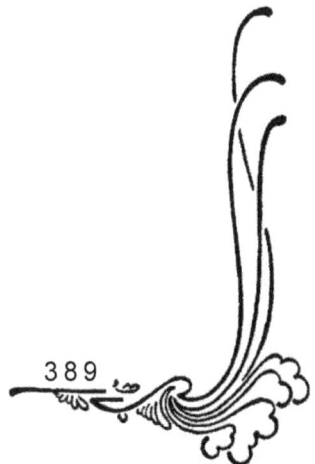

∞

"People
fighting their aloneness
will do almost anything
to avoid silence."

~ Myrtle Barker

∞

"*A bird doesn't sing
because it has an answer,
it sings
because it has a song."*

~ Lou Holtz

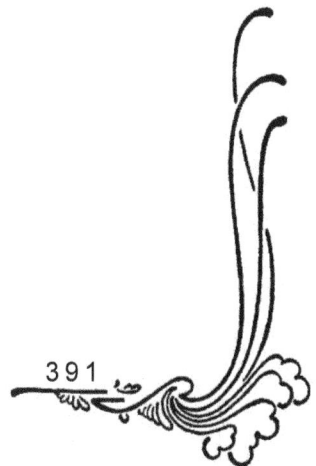

"There are no passengers
on Spaceship Earth.
We are all crew."

~ Marshall McLuhan

"*Let there be spaces
in your togetherness.*"

~ Kahlil Gibran

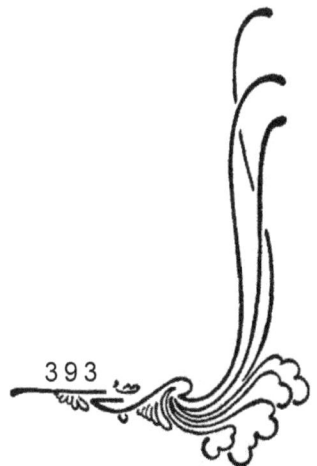

∞

"You'll always miss
100% of the shots
you don't take."

~ Wayne Gretzky

∞

"You can tell
the greatness of a person
by what makes him angry."

~ Abraham Lincoln

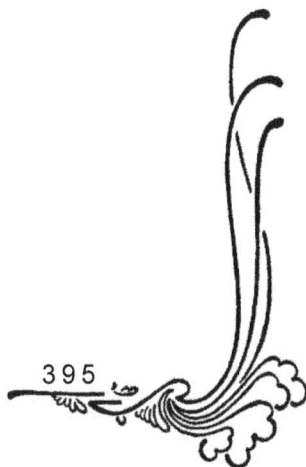

"Smile and wink
at someone today
in a friendly manner.
Help spread a wave
of goodwill and friendship!"

~ Brent N. Hunter

"Since you alone are
responsible for your thoughts,
only you can change them."

~ Paramahansa Yogananda

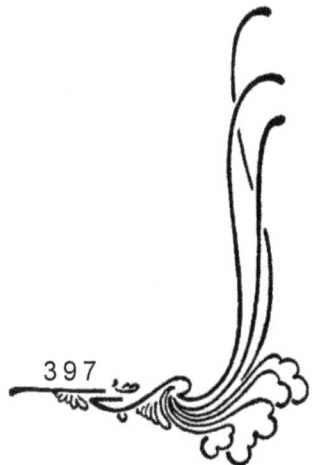

∞

"The only place success
comes before work
is in the dictionary."

~ Vince Lombardi

∞

"*Our attitude towards others determines their attitude towards us.*"

~ Earl Nightingale

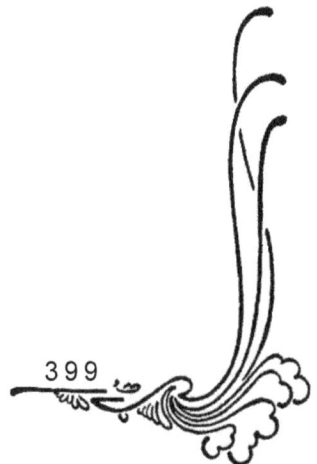

∞

"Enthusiasm
can turn pessimists
into optimists,
losers into winners
and average people
into champions."

~ Reed Markham

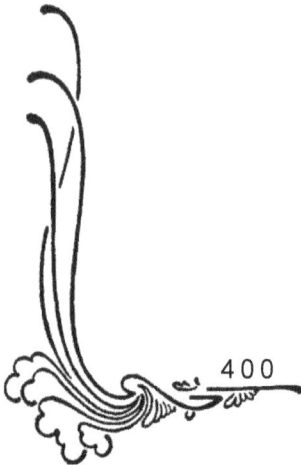

"We could never learn
to be brave or patient
if there were only joys
in the world."

~ Helen Keller

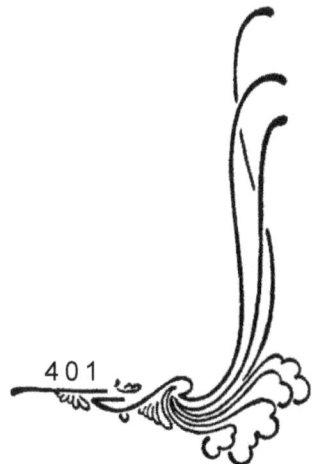

"I learned that courage is not the absence of fear, but the triumph over it."

~ Nelson Mandela

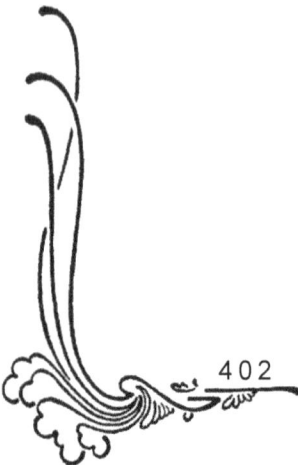

∞

"*Effort only fully releases*
its reward
after a person refuses to quit."

~ Napoleon Hill

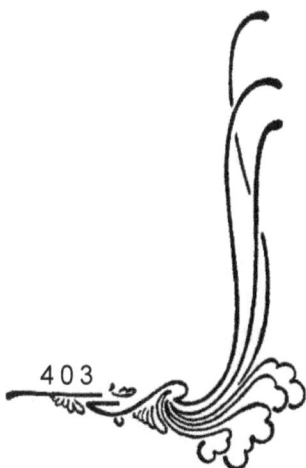

∞

*"Too many of us
are not living our dreams
because we are living
our fears."*

~ Les Brown

"*Build a bridge before the river swells.*"

~ Thangtong Gyalpo

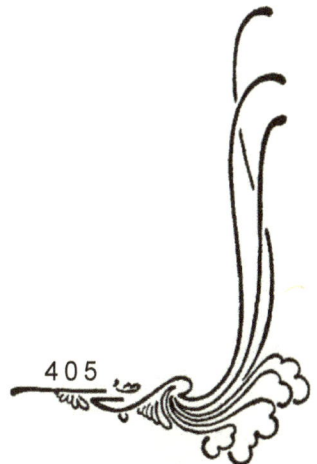

∞

"*If you are irritated
by every rub,
how will your mirror
be polished?*"

~ Jalāl ad-Dīn Muhammad Balkhī "Rumi"

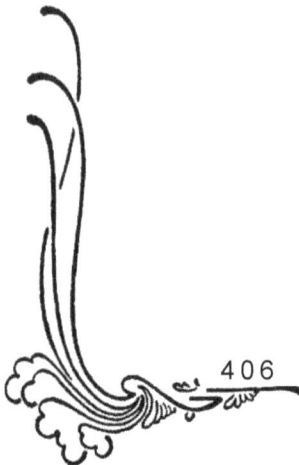

∞

"They can
because they think they can."

~ Virgil

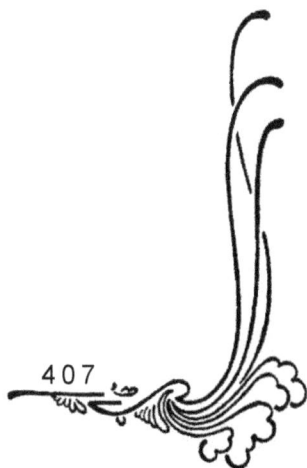

"The most important thing
in communication
is to hear
what isn't being said."

~ Peter Drucker

∞

"No matter what accomplishments you make, somebody helped you."

~ Althea Gibson

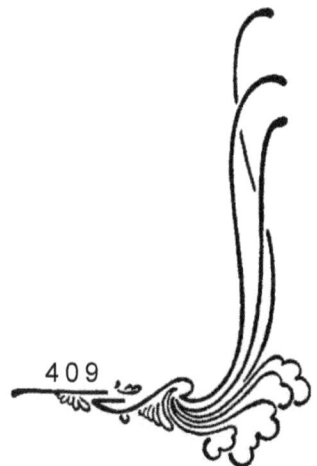

∞

409

"The future starts today,
not tomorrow."

~ Pope John Paul II

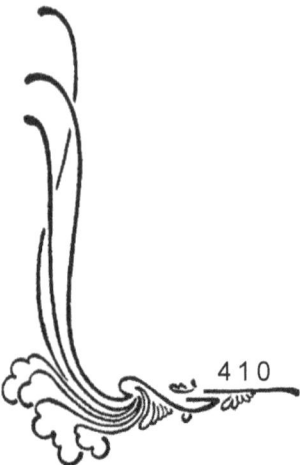

"*Time you enjoy wasting
is not wasted.*"

~ John Lennon

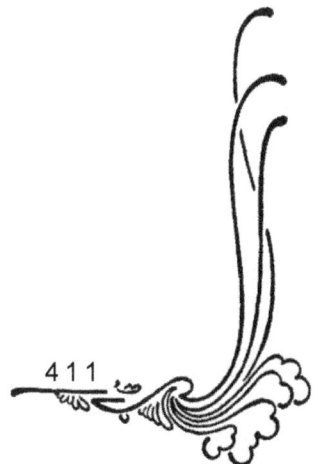

"There comes a moment
when you have to stop
revving up the car
and shove it into gear."

~ David Mahoney

∞

"The cave
you fear to enter
holds the treasure you seek."

~ Joseph Campbell

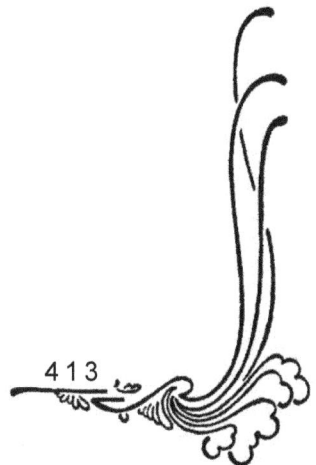

∞

"Be kind and merciful.
Let no one ever come to you
without coming away
better and happier."

~ Mother Teresa

∞

"*Logic will take you from A to B. Imagination will take you everywhere.*"

~ Albert Einstein

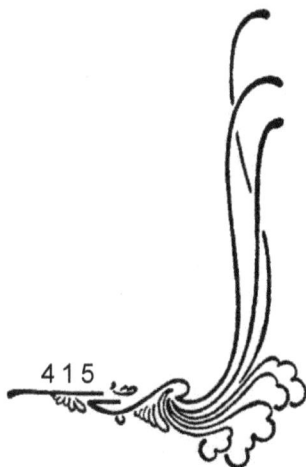

∞

"Don't wish it were easier;
wish you were better."

~ Jim Rohn

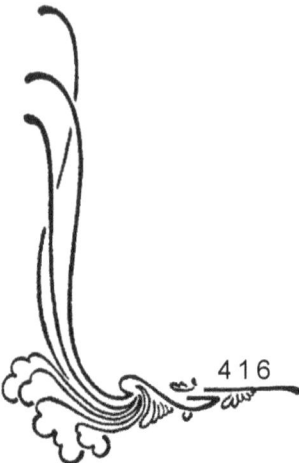

416

"The brick walls
aren't there to keep us out,
they are there to give us
a chance to show how badly
we want something."

~ Randy Pausch

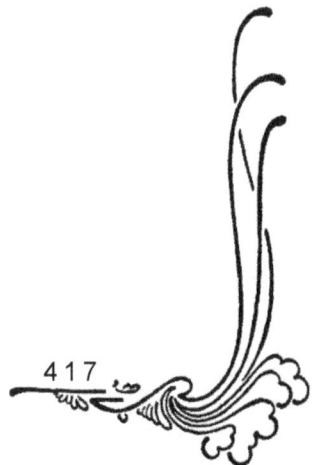

417

"We are called
human beings,
not human doings.
It's who you are,
not what you do
that matters."

~ Rick Warren

"*It is our light,
not our darkness,
that most frightens us.*"

~ Marianne Williamson

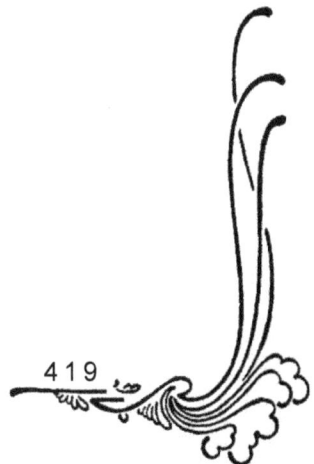

∞

419

"*Most people
never run far enough
on their first wind
to find out
they've got a second wind.*"

~ William James

∞

"The more man meditates
upon good thoughts, the better
will be his world and the
world at large."

~ Confucius

421

"Freedom isn't the goal
of the journey...
it's where the journey begins."

~ Krishnamurti

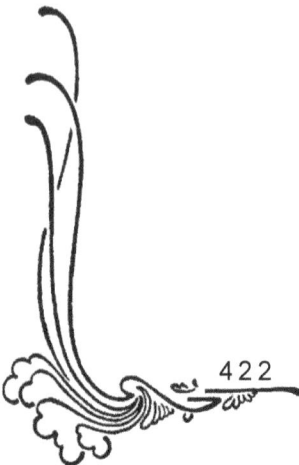

∞

"Even if you are
on the right track,
you will get run over
if you just sit there."

~ Will Rogers

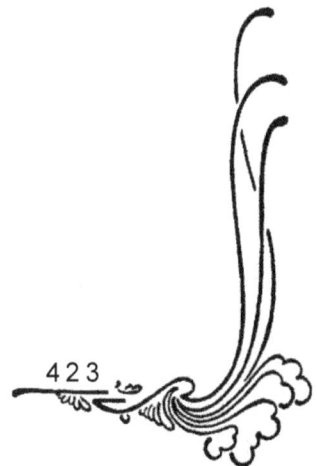

423

*"Life shrinks or expands
in proportion
to one's courage."*

~ Anaïs Nin

424

"*He who binds himself*
to joy,
does the winged life destroy.
But he who kisses the joy
as it flies,
lives in eternity's sunrise."

~ William Blake

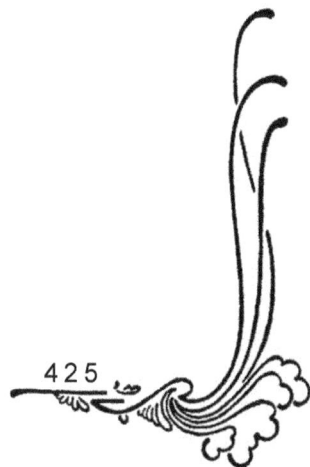

∞

"It is not the strongest
of the species that survives,
nor the most intelligent,
but the one most responsive
to change."

~ Charles Darwin

∞

"*Mother is the word for God on the lips and hearts of all children.*"

~ James O'Barr

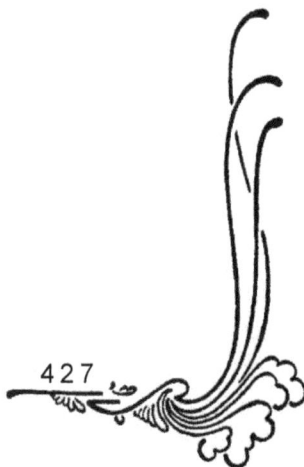

"*Age does not protect
you from love.
But love, to some extent,
protects you from age.*"

~ Jeanne Moreau

∞

"May your joys
be as bright as the morning,
and your sorrows
merely be shadows
that fade in the sunlight
of love."

~ Irish Blessing

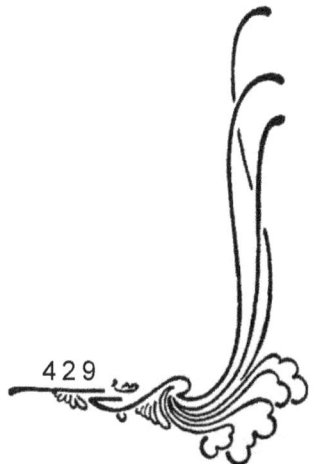

∞

"It takes a team
to build a dream."

~ Anonymous

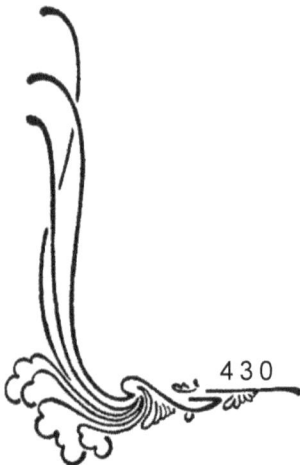

430

"A gem cannot be polished
without friction,
nor a man perfected
without trials."

~ Chinese Proverb

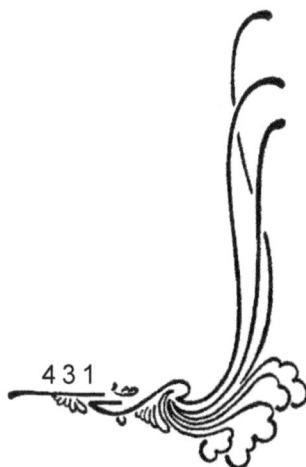

∞

"*Respect others
and others will respect you.*"

~ Confucius

"It isn't
where you came from;
it's where you're going
that counts."

~ Ella Fitzgerald

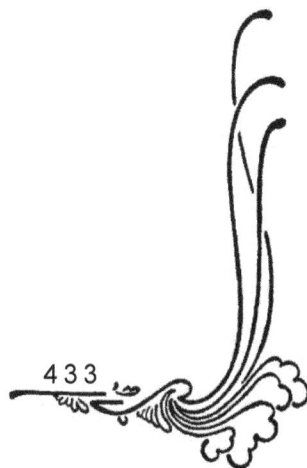

∞

433

"Without faith,
nothing is possible.
With it,
nothing is impossible."

~ Mary Bethune

"Ninety percent
of all those who fail
are not actually defeated.
They simply quit."

~ Paul J. Meyer

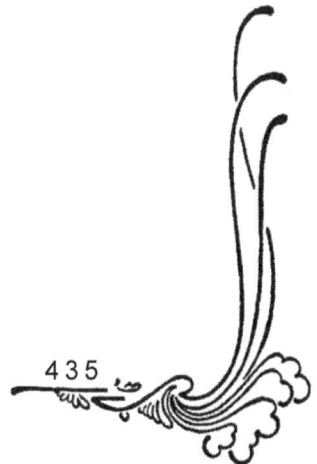

435

"All that is necessary
to break the spell of inertia
and frustration is this:
Act as if
it were impossible to fail."

~ Dorothea Brande

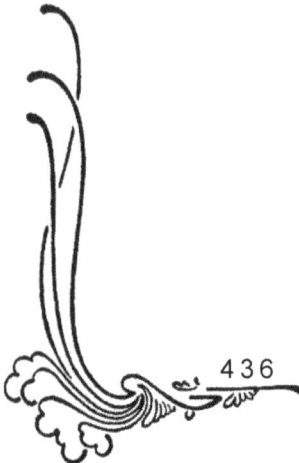

"*Everything should be made as simple as possible, but not simpler.*"

~ Albert Einstein

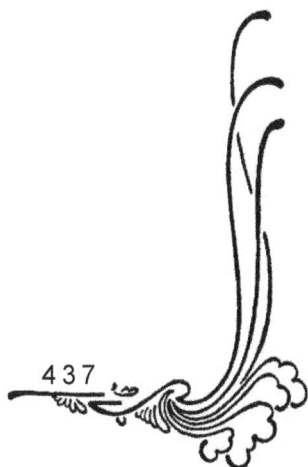

∞

"Success is not final;
failure is not fatal:
it is the courage to continue
that counts."

~ Sir Winston Churchill

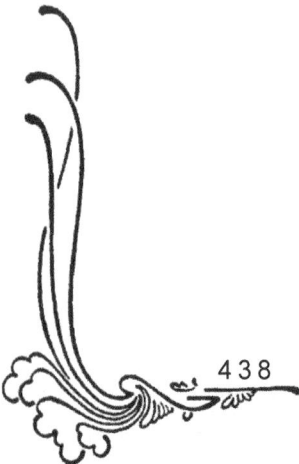

∞

"*All* we see or seem
is but a dream
within a dream."

~ Edgar Allen Poe

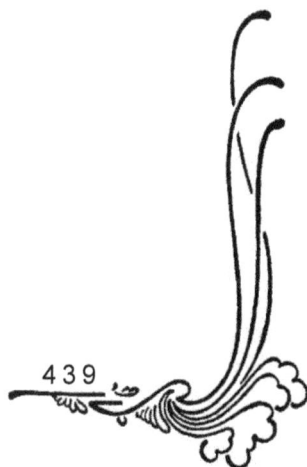

∞

"Doubt is a pain
too lonely to know
that faith is his twin brother."

~ Kahlil Gibran

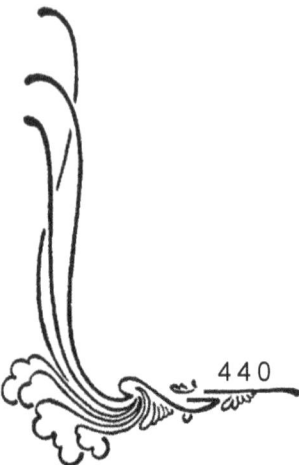

∞

440

"Men are disturbed
not by things that happen,
but by their opinion
of the things that happen."

~ Epictetus

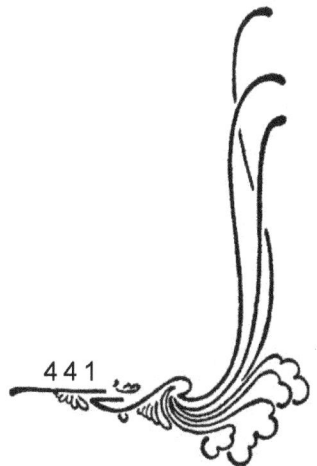

"The snow goose need not
bathe to make itself white.
Neither need you
do anything but be yourself."

~ Lao Tzu

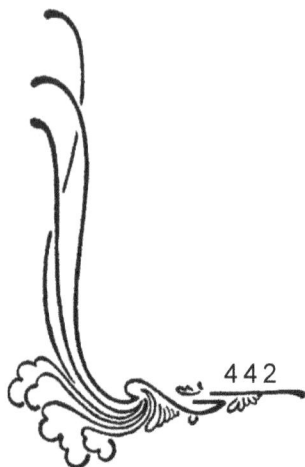

"Yesterday's home runs
don't win today's games."

~ Babe Ruth

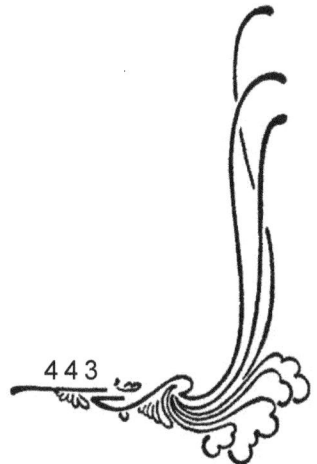

"The only way around
is through."

~ Robert Frost

444

"You have brains
in your head.
You have feet in your shoes.
You can steer yourself,
any direction you choose."

~ Dr. Seuss

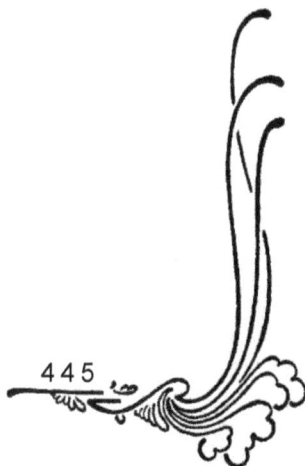

"Genius
is one percent inspiration
and ninety-nine percent
perspiration."

~ Thomas A. Edison

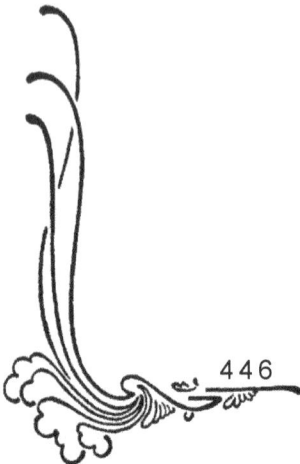

∞

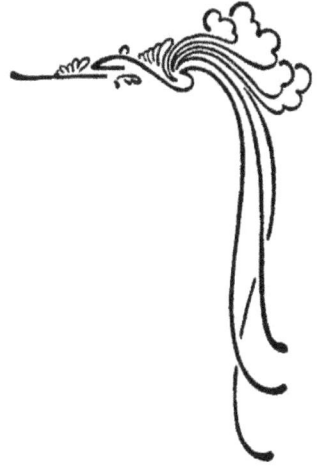

"If I had a single flower
for every time
I think about you,
I could walk forever
in my garden."

~ Unknown

"He who has begun
is half done.
Dare to be wise; begin!"

~ Horace

448

"A great flame follows
a little spark."

~ Dante Alighieri

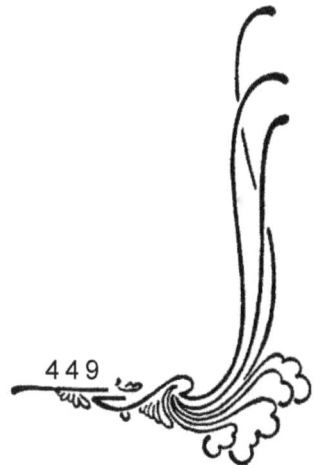

"The happiness of your life
depends on the quality
of your thoughts.
Therefore,
guard accordingly."

~ Marcus Aurelius

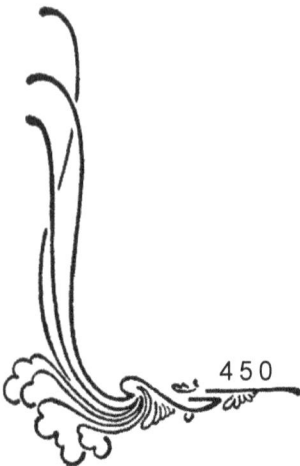

∞

About The Author

Brent Hunter is an author, social media pioneer, IT professional, and certified project manager who uses social media to help inspire and uplift in the spirit of international friendship.

Hunter graduated with a BS in Math and Computer Science from Clarkson University, an MS in Counseling and Human Relations from Villanova University, and the equivalent of an MS in Information Systems as a graduate of the fast-track General Electric Information Systems Management Program. Throughout his career, he has been involved in information technology and security for such notable companies as Blue Shield, Wells Fargo Bank, and General Electric. From 1994 to 2001, Mr. Hunter envisioned, produced and directed the web's first and largest all-inclusive, intentional World Community in cyberspace, The Park.

Hunter's first book, published in 1993, was titled *The Pieces of Our Puzzle* and provided a holistic synthesis of the world's major schools of psychology. Hunter's second book, *The Rainbow Bridge: Bridge to Inner Peace and to World Peace*, illuminates the common ground in the world's major wisdom traditions, also known as universal principles. *The Rainbow Bridge* is the recipient of the Living Now 2013 Bronze Medal for World Peace. Hunter's third book, *Nuggets of Wisdom*, is a companion to this book and contains quotes that are designed to inspire, uplift and empower readers during these times of great change.

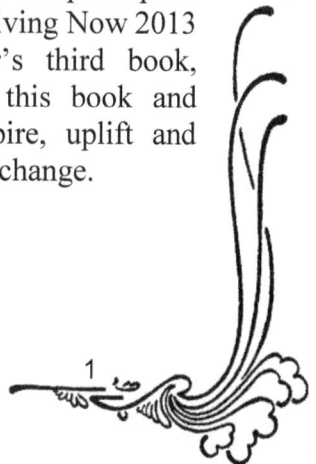

∞

www.ingramcontent.com/pod-product-compliance
Lightning Source LLC
Chambersburg PA
CBHW020752300326
41914CB00050B/167